D1535683

Making the Transition
to Classroom Success

Making the Transition to Classroom Success

Culturally Responsive Teaching for Struggling Language Learners

Helaine W. Marshall, Ph.D.
Long Island University

Andrea DeCapua, Ed.D.
Educational Consultant

Ann Arbor
University of Michigan Press

Copyright © by the University of Michigan 2013
All rights reserved
Published in the United States of America
The University of Michigan Press
Manufactured in the United States of America

∞ Printed on acid-free paper

ISBN-13: 978-0-472-03533-5

2016   2015   2014   2013   4   3   2   1

No part of this publication may be reproduced, stored in a retrieval system, or transmitted in any form or by any means, electronic, mechanical, or otherwise, without the written permission of the publisher.

Contents

Acknowledgments

We wish to thank the following colleagues, students, friends, and family members who have been instrumental in helping us with this book. Mary Carpenter, Maria Dove, Alice Dunning, Magda du Preez, Iris Goldberg, Julia Miller, Rebecca Rich, and Jill Watson all read portions of the manuscript and provided meaningful feedback. Carol Antolini, Elaine Annuziata, Joanne Brogan, Jessica Burke, Betty Cicero, Renee Finneran, Nan Frydland, Kathryn Mercury, Edith Ramirez-Lopez, Madeleine Reyes, and Gloria Rodriguez were among the many teachers who graciously let us into their classrooms. We also wish to acknowledge the substantive contributions that Maria Torres Guzman and Geneva Gay each made to our theoretical perspective. We especially thank our editor, Kelly Sippell, for her endless encouragement and expert editing.

We gratefully acknowledge H. K. Marshall, whose insightful comments and revisions also proved invaluable to the final product.

We appreciate the support of Helaine's institution, and especially that of Sylvia Blake, COO of LIU-Hudson.

Introduction

Immigrant adolescent and adult second language learners enter educational and training programs with a wide range of backgrounds and needs. Many of them may progress well and move beyond basic language needs into more advanced programs. However, there is also a large group of second language learners who do not progress smoothly in their language acquisition and who are at risk of dropping out. While there can be several explanations for why some learners struggle in their attempt to master a new language and to accomplish their educational or vocational goals, a great number of them may be struggling due to "cultural dissonance" (Ibarra, 2001). It is this perspective that we adopt in addressing the difficulties faced by this group of learners.

One of the most significant differences within the population of second language learners, hereafter referred to as L2 learners, is the extent of their prior exposure to the Western-style formal educational paradigm in their new classroom setting. Those learners who are familiar and comfortable with the expectations and assumptions of such education, as well as the target language itself, are likely to progress satisfactorily through the courses and levels of their programs, eventually functioning alongside native speakers in school and/or work settings. However, those learners with no, minimal, or limited exposure to formal education generally do not share the expectations and assumptions of their new setting. Thus, it is these learners who are likely to struggle and find themselves confounded by the ways in which the language and content are presented, practiced, and assessed. In addition, their prior knowledge is not the knowledge expected and valued in formal education. Compounding this problem, many educators fail to consider cultural differences in ways of learning and orientations toward learning (DeCapua & Marshall, 2010a; Nieto, 2010). To prevent these learners from feeling so overwhelmed that they disconnect and turn away from education, institutions and teachers must tailor their instruction to the specific populations enrolled in a given program (Zacarian & Haynes, 2012).

This book, *Making the Transition to Classroom Success: Culturally Responsive Teaching for Struggling Language Learners*, focuses on these struggling L2 learners and examines how understanding their learning paradigm, rooted deeply in their past experiences and cultural orientations, provides a key to the solution to this lack of progress. *Making the Transition* builds on and expands on two of our earlier books, *Meeting the Needs of Students with Limited or Interrupted Formal*

Schooling: A Guide for Educators (2009) and *Breaking New Ground: Teaching Students with Limited or Interrupted Formal Education in U.S. Secondary Schools* (2011). These previous books focused specifically on a subset of struggling L2 learners, those with limited or interrupted formal education (SLIFE) in secondary schools in the U.S. *Meeting the Needs* is a handbook for teachers and administrators of SLIFE, while *Breaking New Ground* introduces, explains, and demonstrates specific applications of our instructional model, the Mutually Adaptive Learning Paradigm (MALP). *Making the Transition to Classroom Success* expands our work to assist teachers working with *all* struggling L2 learners, both adolescents and adults.

Our theoretical framework and instructional model come from the tradition of Culturally Responsive Teaching (CRT). This tradition encourages us to question the relationships among the students, ourselves as teachers, the school curriculum, the school, and society as a whole. What it does not do is "exoticize diverse students as 'other'" (Ladson-Billings, 1995, p. 483). The three major tenets of culturally relevant pedagogy are: conceptions of self and students; social relations; and perceptions of knowledge (Ladson-Billings, 2009). CRT argues that to reach their diverse populations, teachers must develop awareness of the many assumptions they make based on their own cultural orientations, assumptions that one normally does not need to focus on for students who share mainstream experience and backgrounds. We believe it essential that educators understand how *cultural* values, beliefs, and practices influence *educational* beliefs and practices.

CRT uses as a starting point the "cultural characteristics, experiences, and perspectives of ethnically diverse students as conduits for teaching them more effectively" (Gay, 2002, 106). Doing so makes learning more meaningful to such students, leading to higher achievement. Gay identifies five areas where teachers need to have expertise in order to implement CRT: (1) developing a cultural diversity knowledge base that includes both content knowledge and pedagogical skills; (2) developing a culturally relevant curriculum and instructional strategies; (3) demonstrating cultural caring and building a learning community; (4) understanding the dynamics of cross-cultural communication; and (5) creating cultural congruity in the delivery of classroom instruction. In our work, we have explored these areas with respect to unsuccessful L2 learners, leading us to design an instructional model that addresses their needs and strengths. While our model incorporates all five areas, the primary focus lies in the fifth area, creating cultural congruity, which we see as the weakest in the many classrooms we have observed. The most immediate need for teachers implementing CRT is a roadmap to create this cultural congruity, thereby lessening the cultural dissonance (Ibarra, 2001) many L2 learners may encounter.

In designing this roadmap, we have complemented and extended CRT by introducing a mutually adaptive approach in which the priorities of both the learner and the formal educational setting are taken equally into account. Following CRT, the culture of learners includes more than the visible aspects of culture, which are readily accessible and easily incorporated into instruction. It is the invisible aspects of culture, those that establish the means by which one accesses new knowledge and skills (DeCapua & Wintergerst, 2004; Hall, 1966) that elude superficial examination and require an in-depth analysis.

The struggling L2 learners we address in this book are caught between two worlds: Western-style formal education with its scholastic and literacy expectations and the pragmatic, informal world of their previous learning experiences. Even the most practical, everyday activities, such as taking a written driver's test, require formal components that are anchored in the norms of Western-style learning. The two approaches that most immediately present themselves are: (1) teach according to the learners' assumptions about learning to ensure that they are comfortable and will respond well to instruction; or (2) teach according to the Western model but simplify it, continuing to cover material until learners have mastered it so that the learners are exposed to what is required of them in their new setting. The first approach, while laudable in the short term and culturally responsive, ultimately will not result in their success in the system. To move forward in a system of formal education, all learners must perform and be assessed in the Western-style in order to earn credentials, diplomas, or certificates. The second approach, in practice the more common one, while designed to result in eventual academic success, in fact results in what is referred to as an "achievement gap." Many L2 learners can make progress through this approach, but others, because they cannot rely on any of their own ways of learning, continue to struggle. Their progress is minimal or at least slower than expected; therefore, both they and their teachers can become quite frustrated. For these learners, teachers continue to simplify the material and reteach it, which perpetuates the Western-style educational paradigm. When they still don't get results, teachers conclude that the students cannot learn the material. At the same time, students, not seeing tangible results, become disenchanted with schooling and/or the programs and often drop out.

Calls for CRT have encouraged teachers, teacher trainers, and administrators to work toward bridging the gap between the two approaches by incorporating the lives of the students and their cultural knowledge, as well as community resources, into classroom settings. Efforts in many different areas of the world have demonstrated the effectiveness of developing and implementing CRT strategies, pedagogy, curriculum, and classroom environments in promoting the participation and success of struggling learners (e.g., United Kingdom: Andrews & Yee, 2006; Australia and the United States: Hickling-Hudson & Ahlquist, 2003; India: Guha, 2006; Canada: Kanu, 2007; New Zealand: Sexton; 2011). CRT offers valuable contributions to making curriculum more meaningful and relevant to L2 learners of diverse backgrounds and educational experiences.

The Mutually Adaptive Learning Paradigm, or MALP (Marshall, 1994, 1998), extensively described in our book *Breaking New Ground* (DeCapua & Marshall, 2011), provides a framework for teaching that transitions struggling L2 learners from their preferred and customary ways of learning to Western-style formal education. The goal here is to use a strong theoretical foundation from CRT to create an intercultural framework, the Intercultural Communication Framework (ICF), and to expand on MALP so that instructors have a concrete, practical set of guidelines to follow in designing and delivering instruction to struggling L2 learners. The MALP model embraces key assumptions about learning held by L2 learners who struggle as a result of cultural dissonance and places them into a framework that also integrates key elements of Western-style education. The resulting mutually adaptive learning paradigm serves as a roadmap for teachers as they incorporate knowledge and understanding of the expectations of such learners into their pedagogy.

We believe that all adolescent and adult learners who want to participate in the new culture need to adjust to the different expectations they encounter in school settings. Adolescent learners often think of themselves as adults and commonly arrive in their new nation expecting to be considered as such. Their prior (and even current) experiences often include adult lives out of school and in their society. Whether the struggling L2 learner attends a program in a secondary school setting or in an adult educational setting, the issues faced regarding Western-style formal education remain the same. The remedies for the learners in both settings are similar and can be implemented appropriately for the specific context and program of those learners.

Although there are myriad issues related to the lack of progress by this student population, we focus solely on pedagogy; issues outside the teacher's control, such as economic concerns and matters of policy, are beyond the scope of this book. (See, however, Bigelow, 2010; Cummins, Brown, & Sayers, 2007; Freeman & Freeman, 2002; Mencken, 2008.)

In *Making the Transition to Classroom Success*, we explore cultural differences and pedagogical implications, within the context of a continuum of the ways of learning and teaching. We begin by considering both Western-style formal education and informal learning, follow with an exploration of the Ways of Learning Continuum, and then examine the cultural aspects of individualism and collectivism and their impact on assumptions about teaching and learning.

The first two chapters concentrate on culture and its implications for education and communication. Chapter 1 explores the foundation of culture and how it relates to learning in the tradition of CRT. Chapter 2 builds on this and presents the theoretical framework for the approach taken in the book, the Intercultural Communication Framework, and its guiding principles.

The following three chapters present the instructional model, MALP. Chapter 3 outlines the model and describes its key elements. Chapter 4 is devoted to the most challenging element of MALP, scaffolding ways of thinking and responding derived from basic tenets of formal education. Chapter 5 presents steps to follow in creating a project using the model and gives examples and analysis of one project.

The next two chapters describe what MALP looks like in terms of the instruction itself. In Chapter 6, we move into the classroom to observe and describe the delivery of instruction guided by MALP and introduce the flipped classroom as a possible means for enhancing learning opportunities. Chapter 7 continues the examination of a MALP classroom by exploring the physical environment, including material on the classroom walls, available resources and equipment, and arrangement of furniture.

The final chapter, Chapter 8, presents the MALP Implementation Rubric designed for an assessment of MALP in the classroom. At the conclusion of this book, teachers should feel competent to implement the model and assess their implementation.

1

Culture and Learning

Curriculum theorist James MacDonald once quoted Einstein's question, "What does a fish know about the water in which he spends his life?" (MacDonald, 1988, p. 102). It is not a question that typically appears in educational discourse, yet the matter it addresses—what counts as and is assessed as knowledge—is at the very core of what it means to engage in the practice of education. Watson (2010) has interpreted Einstein's question in an anecdote that frames our discussion of culture and learning:

> From the literate scientist perspective, the fish knows nothing about water, not the chemical formula, not the temperature of freezing and boiling, not how to purify water or mix it with other substances, nor any of the scientific minutiae that are the province of hydrologists. From the oral indigenous perspective, the fish lives and breathes water, is enveloped by water, is born, finds a mate, gives birth in, and dies in water. A fish knows how to navigate water, sensing and responding to its slightest undulations every minute of its life. No one knows more about water than a fish. The difference is precisely to what extent knowledge is conceived as empathetic and participatory as opposed to something one has or wields from a state of separation. Both kinds may be considered knowledge, but not of the same thing, and not with the same costs and consequences. (p. 178)

Effective teaching for ethnically diverse students emanates from a deep understanding of various perspectives on learning, teaching, and knowledge and an ability to accommodate them in a classroom setting. Our pedagogical approach is grounded in the tradition of Culturally Responsive Teaching (CRT) as advocated by Gay (2000; 2002) and Ladson-Billings (1994; 1995), among others. Following CRT, academic knowledge and skills derived from Western-style formal education must be situated within the lived experiences and frames of references of students who come from different ways of learning and teaching.

1

Ways of Learning

Western-Style Formal Education and Informal Learning

The education that is provided in most European-American industrialized societies is known as Western-style formal education. This type of education, although not universal, has become prevalent throughout the world, often accompanied by cultural adaptations to suit the specific country of its implementation (Anderson-Levitt, 2003; Grigorenko, 2007). The underpinnings of Western-style formal education include scientific reasoning, observation, and logical deduction. As dictated by this foundation, the focus of such education is using the scientific method to arrive at facts, gaining an understanding of these facts, and finally ordering, classifying or, in some other way, making sense of these facts (Flynn, 2007; Ozmon & Carver, 2008). Moreover, learning is centered on teaching through abstract concepts removed from daily life and experience, didactic pedagogy, testing by examinations and closely associated with literacy, written media, and print resources. Finally, the settings for such learning generally consist of formal schools where trained teachers deliver pre-determined curricula. A salient characteristic of this type of learning is decontextualized learning—that is, learning that "is removed from the immediate context of socially relevant action" (Bruner, 1961, p. 62).

Informal learning, in contrast, is commonly seen as occurring naturally, as part of daily life, and is based on the sociocultural practices of a community. It is like the fish's knowledge of water in the introductory anecdote. Informal learning results from family or community members teaching children life skills to help them become successful adults. Even very young children experience informal learning when they engage in on-the-job training and apprenticing in endeavors important to the family and community, such as helping with the weaving, hoeing, herding, laundry, childcare, various farm chores, and/or participating in religious events. In these endeavors, the mastery of essential skills, techniques, and procedures important in everyday life, rather than learning per se, constitute the focus and the goals. Informal learning predominates in traditional cultures where children perform tasks and engage in activities central to their families and communities, as well as in subcultures that may not have access to Western-style formal education (Paradise & Rogoff, 2009). It is important to note that these informal experiences, while not taking place in a school setting, nonetheless result in learning. Such learning can be thought of as an alternative way of learning, distinct from the way of learning required in formal school settings.

We now examine these two ways of learning in more detail by identifying key characteristics that differentiate them.

Immediate Relevance and Pragmatic Tasks

As noted, *informal learning does not take place in classrooms with trained teachers but instead is focused on the activities and tasks of daily life and therefore has immediate relevance.* In many cultures across the world where informal learning predominates, learning is intimately tied to the land, its ecology, and the constantly evolving transmitted knowledge of its inhabitants (Battiste & Henderson, 2000). Fulani children in West Africa, for example, actively take part in family and community spheres of labor from a very young age. By age six, daughters learn how to pound grain and weave; at about four or five years of age, boys receive a calf of their own to take care of and which will later form the basis of their own herd (Johnson, 2000). Quechua children, both boys and girls, care for younger siblings by the age of four. At about the same age girls engage in household tasks and boys work in the fields and with animals (Tenebaum, Visscher, Pons, & Harris, 2004). In Guatemala City, as in many urban centers in developing countries, children enter the workforce early, selling goods, working as maids, working in the tourist industry, and in other jobs (Offit, 2008). Children are not isolated from adult spheres of work. They observe, imitate, and practice pragmatic tasks alongside adults; what they learn has immediate results, applications, or consequences. In this context, there is little use for reading or writing. Literacy skills are viewed as nonessential, even peripheral, to learning. The priority is the effective realization of a pragmatic task in pursuit of the immediately relevant: the necessities, demands, obligations, and pleasures of everyday life.

In contrast, *formal education implicitly emphasizes future relevance.* For example, learning geometry, social studies, or science may not have immediate application, but it does serve to further cognitive development to prepare students for more education and, later, for more skilled careers. In addition, as previously noted, Western-style formal education trains students from an early age in ways of thinking that reflect academic concepts and decontextualized tasks grounded in the precepts of formal education. Learning is understood as the gradual accumulation of knowledge that serves to help students build a knowledge base for pathways and connections to future learning.

A well regarded taxonomy of the ways of thinking is that of Bloom (1956), revised by Anderson & Krathwohl (2001) and relied on by educators in designing curriculum and teaching materials to develop the critical-thinking skills considered essential in formal education settings (Kuhn, 2009). The taxonomy presents six levels of cognition, with lower-order thinking skills at the bottom—

that is, thinking processes such as *remembering* that require less complex thinking than those closer to the top of the hierarchy, such as *analyzing*. The lower-order thinking skills are primarily concerned with accessing and retaining information, while the higher-order thinking skills are seen as more complex because they are associated with examining, evaluating, and incorporating information. It is higher-order skills of thinking that are the *sine qua non* of Western-style formal education worldwide.

Interconnectedness and Shared Responsibility

In our examination of the ways of learning, we need to refer to a cultural construct, *collectivism*. Cultures that can be labeled collectivistic emphasize the interdependence of individuals and their relationship to others in the pursuit of shared goals and interests. These relationships include family solidarity and obligations but extend as well to a wider network of kinship, community, ethnic, religious, and other groups. There is a strong sense of accountability and responsibility to the members of one's groups, as well as respect for elders and those in positions of power vis-à-vis oneself. The majority of cultures around the world are collectivistic (Triandis, 1995).

Latinos, the largest growing immigrant population in the U.S. (Pew Research Center Hispanic Report, 2013), tend toward collectivism, emphasizing respect for and politeness to adults and the importance of the extended family (Peña & Mendez-Perez, 2006; Rodriguez & Olswang, 2003). In Latino families, for example, children helping their parents and other siblings and family members may be as much a priority as regular school attendance or homework. This orientation, far from being limited to Latino cultures by any means, is found among many immigrants coming from collectivistic cultures around the world (see, e.g., Fuligini, Tseng, & Lam, 1999; Gahungu, Gahungu, & Lusano, 2011; Yeh, Kim, Pituc, & Atkins, 2008).

A collectivistic orientation also inclines members of these cultures to engage collaboratively in learning, minimizing individual roles, individual achievement, and individual accountability (Rothstein-Fisch & Trumbull, 2008). A strong sense of shared responsibility is the norm for this population. The group works together; who performs each specific task is not as important as the completion of the job or the assignment. This understanding assumes that everyone has something to contribute, regardless of level of expertise, and will do so when appropriate as the situation unfolds. A collectivistic orientation does not, however, preclude individual effort or achievement. Members of collectivistic cultures often strive to succeed individually; however, their motivation in such is not to excel as an individual but rather as a representative of the group to which they owe allegiance and to which they hope to bring pride and satisfaction in their individual achievements (Hofstede, Hofstede, & Minkov, 2010). The Chinese, for instance, are a very collectivistic culture known for their emphasis on individual scholastic achievement, which confers honor and success on families as a whole. In collectivistic cultures, the focus remains the group and one's loyalty to the group as opposed to personal self-actualization.

An *individualistic* orientation, in contrast, focuses on each person and what that person alone can achieve. Members of such cultures prefer to act and see themselves as individuals. Independence, rather than interdependence, is fostered, and self-reliance, personal achievement, and the rights of individuals are stressed. North America, Australia, Great Britain, and Germany are examples of individualistic cultures that stress the autonomy of the individual in the pursuit of personal goals and interests. Individual desires are the priority, and decisions are based on personal preferences (Hofstede, Hofstede, & Minkov, 2010; Hofstede & McCrae, 2004). This emphasis on individualism is reflected in teaching styles and texts prevalent in mainstream classrooms and promoted even in the earliest stages of schooling where children are encouraged to make their own decisions and move toward independent learning (see, e.g., Estes, Mintz, & Gunter, 2011; Joyce, Weil, & Calhoun, 2009). Even the emphasis on "higher-order critical thinking skills" (Anderson & Krathwohl, 2001; Bloom, 1956) where, for example, students are expected to take issues and explore different sides, reflects individualistic values rather than the group consensus or deference to authority typically preferred in collectivistic cultures (Hsu, 1985).

Although we have presented the notions of individualism and collectivism as a dichotomy, in reality, cultures range along a continuum of more or less individualistic or collectivistic. In addition, within any given majority culture, there are various subcultures that vary in their individualistic-collectivistic orientations. Although all cultures are collections of individuals who themselves may exhibit varying degrees of such behaviors, the differences lie primarily in the degree to which or how much individuals reflect the dominant values of their group (DeCapua & Marshall, 2011; Oyserman & Lee, 2008; Triandis, 2000).

Oral Transmission and Oral Traditions

As we describe the ways of learning, we must address the factor of literacy because Western-style formal education is premised on extracting and transmitting meaning via print (Eisenstein, 1979). Informal learning is primarily oral, with limited or no emphasis on literacy. Yet, even in cultures where informal learning is the norm, there is a wide range of literacy experiences. Some people may have never been exposed to literacy because their language may have no written form, or have only recently been codified, or there may be few or no resources available in their native language (Schwieter & Jaimes-Domínguez, 2009). In Mexico, for example, while the official language is Spanish, there are 68 different languages spoken by indigenous communities for which there are limited, if any, print resources (Rockwell & Gomes, 2009). In many areas of the world, access to schooling may be restricted to elites, and materials to support education may be a scarce commodity (Illich, 1973). Some people may have limited abilities relevant to their age and/or grade and, for some, literacy may not be of importance (McBrien, 2011; Whitescarver & Kalman, 2009) because it is not perceived as relevant to people's daily lives or it may only have limited utilitarian uses. They may see literacy as useful or necessary for specific tasks—such as reading bus tickets, medicine labels, church bulletins, store advertisements, fast food menus, or directions for video games, or for obtaining official documents— but do not view literacy as a process by which to gain and transmit information (Dyer & Choksi, 2001; Sarroub, Pernicek, & Sweeney, 2007; Zubair, 2001). In all instances, the priority is exchanging and extracting most or all information via oral modes rather than print modes. Orality is a way of life.

Despite having limited or no literacy, these people are successful participants in their own social contexts and the sociocultural practices of their cultures. They have strong oral skills and can often recite long texts from memory, such as poetry, stories, written religious texts, or other works (Bigelow, 2010). In industrialized societies, however, literacy is essential to effective participation and engagement in the community and limited literacy presents social and economic challenges (Bernardo, 2003). In formal education, a key institution in such a society, literacy is essential. Extracting meaning from print and producing written texts form the core of learning. Adolescents and adults without appropriate literacy are viewed by many educators as deficient and less capable than those with such skills (Valenzuela, 1999). Students are introduced to basic literacy skills in the first years of schooling, and by the time of adolescence and adulthood, print literacy is assumed.

As this discussion illustrates, there is a divide between informal learning and Western-style formal education. On the one hand, informal learning is oriented to a pragmatic, oral perspective, while Western-style formal education is oriented to an academic, literate perspective. In addition, while Western-style formal education tends to espouse individual accountability, most cultures of the world are more collectivistic than individualistic.

In this book we address L2 learners who are struggling in formal Western-style classrooms. These learners often lack age-appropriate literacy skills and are somewhere on the continuum between orality and literacy. They still prefer the oral mode and find the prescribed use of literacy as the basis for learning arduous and unnatural. Even after extended exposure to literacy, for many their preferred mode of communication remains oral and literacy remains problematic (Bigelow, 2010; Souryasack & Lee, 2007). We continue our discussion by examining who struggling L2 learners are and the difficulties they encounter in Western-style formal educational settings.

Ways of Learning Continuum

Critically important to understanding the ways of learning is to envision the differences in terms of a continuum, first introduced in DeCapua & Marshall (2011) and expanded now in this book. Figure 1.1 illustrates this continuum, with oral transmission and informal learning placed at the left end of the continuum and Western-style formal education and literacy on the right end. We understand the ways of learning as a continuum and not a dichotomy because struggling L2 learners differ in how much previous exposure they may have had to formal education and how far they have transitioned to this type of education.

FIGURE 1.1 Ways of Learning Continuum

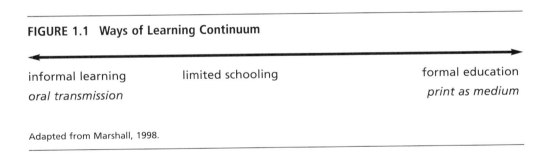

informal learning   limited schooling   formal education
oral transmission   *print as medium*

Adapted from Marshall, 1998.

This continuum provides a lens for examining students entering the formal educational system to determine their level of exposure, familiarity, and success in that system. Although many L2 learners come to a new country with a background in formal education in their native country, many also arrive with limited or no schooling. It is important to distinguish, however, between students who come from strictly oral cultures and have no experience in schools and those who have participated in some schooling but have considered it a struggle. It is the group of students who have started to move to the right side of the continuum that often become neglected. They may be viewed as lacking in ability because they have had an opportunity to demonstrate their ability and have not been successful. We call this group *struggling L2 learners* and devote our energies to outlining an approach that will reach them and result in their ultimate achievement in formal education settings.

Struggling Adolescent and Adult L2 Learners

L2 learners in general are adapting to a new language and culture because they are learning in a new setting and their native language and culture is not the basis for instruction. Many L2 learners are able to concentrate on the new language, new subject matter content, and/or workplace skills. They are already familiar with Western-style formal educational norms, and they can leverage that familiarity, transferring their learning behaviors to the new setting. However, other L2 learners do not progress in their learning. We use the term *struggling L2 learners* to refer to these students who, for whatever reason, do not respond to instruction and do not achieve success as defined in the system in which they find themselves. Specifically, we focus on the subset of L2 adolescents and adult learners who struggle as a result of cultural differences between their own expectations and practices and those of Western-style formal education. We are not addressing those students who may struggle as a result of having learning disabilities.

Struggling L2 learners will fall somewhere toward the left of the continuum. The first type of struggling learner is the student with limited or interrupted formal education, known as SLIFE (DeCapua & Marshall, 2011; DeCapua, Smathers, & Tang, 2009). While some may have their first exposure to literacy and schooling when they enter schools in the industrialized world, others may have had some exposure to schooling, albeit limited. By *limited* we mean that their education has been interrupted because of war, relocation, migration, or other reasons, or that their schooling does not meet the requisite grade- and/or age-level expectations of formal education. Such schooling may have been primarily religious-based, lacked basic resources and/or trained teachers, or may have consisted of specialized programs that met specific needs, including training in better farming practices, family health practices, and the like.

Another common type of struggling L2 learner is the student who has managed, due to oral proficiency and social integration with peers in the new setting, to appear to be simply less capable. It is this group in particular that avoids classroom interactions and is often under the radar until encountering a placement test or achievement test demanding reading and writing skills of an academic nature. In both adolescent and adult classroom settings, these are the L2 learners who tend to repeat grades or program levels and yet can converse in the new language and manage in their local communities. We submit that these struggling L2 learners, despite their success in other culturally different settings, are, in fact, experiencing extreme cultural dissonance in the school setting itself. By *cultural dissonance* we are referring to the sense of confusion and dislocation that students coming from different cultural backgrounds and ways of learning experience when confronted with the expectations and demands of Western-style formal education (Ibarra, 2001; Nieto, 2010).

In all cases, these are learners who are attempting to master an unfamiliar language in a formal education setting that may also be more or less unfamiliar and alienating, depending where they are on the continuum. For these learners, it is not only the language and the setting that are new and foreign, but also they are encountering a different form of thinking and different priorities—academic ways of thinking and literacy. Literacy and formal Western-style education lead to different cognitive processes and priorities (Cole, 2005; Petersson et al., 2000; Tarone & Bigelow, 2005).

What Factors Determine Where Struggling L2 Learners Are on the Continuum?

Since we cannot examine all factors, we examine a few of the more salient ones. Let us begin by considering orality and literacy. Those whose native languages are not codified, or only very recently so, will fall much closer to the left end of the continuum because they have not made the transition to print. Other L2 learners who have basic literacy skills may also fall toward the left end because for them, reading and writing are equated with copying and reciting, or as a means for reproducing meaning. They have made the transition to literacy as a skill, but literacy is not a fully developed concept that allows them to see and use print as a means and resource for accessing and creating meaning. Others who have stronger literacy skills may fall closer to the middle of the continuum, yet still not have transitioned fully to literacy.

Another factor influencing where L2 learners fall on the continuum is their collectivistic-individualistic orientation, and how much this aligns with accepted and expected school practices. When students come with strong notions of shared work and responsibility, it can be difficult for them to partici-pate in classes promoting individual work and responsibility. Likewise, students from different ethnic, cultural, religious, and/or socioeconomic groups may have difficulties engaging in collaborative learning practices because they are not accustomed to working together with others who are not of their group. In addition, some learners view group work as less serious and inappropriate in a school setting (Liang, 2004).

Struggling L2 learners, especially those closer to the left end of the continuum, face discrepancies and discord in their ways of learning and in the expected ways of learning of formal schooling. The gulf between the assumptions of most mainstream educators about teaching and learning and those of informal learners is a major contributor to the cultural dissonance these students experience when they find themselves in the classroom. This cultural dissonance is exacerbated by the fact that educators in Western-style formal education are generally unaware of the ways of learning continuum and the influence it exerts on the daily lives of the students in their care. They may also be significantly challenged in their ability to incorporate a culturally responsive approach to instruction into their curriculum and lessons on an everyday basis.

Assumptions about Teaching and Learning

In order to prepare teachers to work with struggling L2 learners, the first step must be to make them aware of the Ways of Learning Continuum and, concomitant with that effort, their assumptions about school and their often unspoken expectations for students. Educators and mainstream participants in formal Western-style educational systems are generally unaware of their own assumptions about teaching and learning because they take these for granted or accept them as a given about education (August, Goldenberg, & Rueda, 2006). As with any set of assumptions, these are below the level of awareness for most teachers and learners—they presume that all learning is based on the assumptions held by those participating in formal education, but, as we have seen, these ways of learning are not universal. To reach struggling L2 learners more effectively, educators should begin by acknowledging their own assumptions, finding out how they differ from those of their students, and then using their understanding of the differences in ways of learning to promote student success in the new setting. Germane at this juncture is an examination of these assumptions. See Figure 1.2.

FIGURE 1.2 Assumptions of Teachers and Learners in Western-Style Formal Education

1. The goals of instruction are to
   a. prepare learners for their future.
   b. produce learners who are individually accountable for their learning.

2. The learner has age-appropriate preparation for
   a. literacy tasks used in accessing and transmitting knowledge.
   b. decontextualized tasks requiring academic ways of thinking.

Adapted from Marshall, 1998; DeCapua & Marshall, 2011.

The first goal of formal Western-style education is to prepare students for their future. Lessons or even units may have immediate applications to students' lives. Overall, however, formal education rests on the premise that what students learn in the classroom is preparation for future learning or the workplace. In addition, formal education holds that students are accountable for their own learning. In collectivistic cultures, this accountability is frequently evident in the emphasis on rigorous high-stakes examination systems where students compete to earn entry to coveted educational institutions to gain prestige, status, and/or respect for their group. In more individualistic cultures, achievement and excellence are encouraged and students are rewarded as deserving individuals (Chung & Mallery, 2000; Greenfield, Quiroz, & Raeff, 2000).

Regarding students' preparation for learning in a classroom setting, educators assume that adolescent and adult students have already developed age-appropriate literacy skills and are reasonably facile with using print resources for extracting and exhibiting knowledge. A review of the literature indicates that this holds true across Western-formal style classrooms around the world (see, e.g., Al-Amoush, et al., 2011; Bulut, 2006; Chitty, 2002). Second, in Western-style formal education, learning is based on the notion that there are specific, scientific ways of organizing knowledge, or academic ways of thinking, that build skills in making the new material the subject of further inquiry, elaboration, evaluation and, in general, analysis. Educators assume that adolescent and adult students have the appropriate preparation to engage in these academic ways of thinking and perform tasks designed to demonstrate mastery.

Most international migration reflects a move from collectivist cultures to more individualistic ones. The United States, for example, is first in the world for receiving immigrants, with top numbers arriving from collectivistic cultures in Latin America and Asia (U.S. Census Bureau, 2012). The United Kingdom

also takes in large numbers of immigrants, again generally from more collectivistic cultures. Thus, we need to consider one more assumption: that the role of
educators is to produce independent learners for an individualistic culture—
that is, students who are capable of using resources and engaging in thinking
skills to access information and extract knowledge necessary for the classroom.
To encourage independent learners, teachers scaffold learning, either implicitly
or explicitly, so that learners develop the ability to engage in independent learning, while encouraging them to compete and excel as individuals.

This assumption is particularly evident in Western-style education in cultures closer to the individualistic end of the collectivistic-individualistic continuum. In more individualistic cultures, particularly in the last several decades,
teachers are viewed more as mentors and facilitators than as authoritarian figures responsible for imparting knowledge to their students (Leung, 2001;
Nisbett, 2003).

As we have seen, these assumptions about teaching and learning do not
necessarily apply to struggling L2 learners. Because struggling L2 learners are
orientated to the left side of the Ways of Learning Continuum, they have a different paradigm of learning with different assumptions about teaching and
learning (DeCapua & Marshall, 2011). When these learners enter Western-style
formal classrooms, they face a major paradigm shift as they move along the continuum from oral transmission and informal learning toward literacy and formal education. Struggling adolescent and adult L2 learners know how to learn
in their familiar context; what this population needs is to shift its learning paradigm, which entails discarding one's previous assumptions in favor of new,
very different ones from those previously held (Kuhn, 1970). By understanding
that these learners are engaging in a paradigm shift in their ways of learning,
educators avoid a deficit viewpoint—that is, focusing on what these learners
lack in contrast to mainstream formally educated students. Furthermore, it is
important that educators realize that one's accustomed ways of learning are
residual and learners are likely to gravitate toward them, even after exposure to
new ways of learning. This is especially true if learners are older when they first
encounter Western-style formal education, as their cognitive structure, condi-
tioned in other ways of learning, is already more advanced in its development
(Cole, 2005; Petersson et al., 2000). It takes a concerted effort and considerable
time for a paradigm shift to occur. To facilitate this paradigm shift, we have proposed the Mutually Adaptive Learning Paradigm (MALP), an instructional
model specifically designed to meet the needs of struggling L2 learners. A
framework for using MALP is the subject of Chapter 2.

2

The Intercultural Communication Framework

Ms. Gonzalves asks, "How can I help my learners begin to connect the 'real' with the 'abstract'? In my classes with beginners, we spend a lot of time using their own experience to present, scaffold, re-scaffold, review, and scaffold again new with old material. I think we can all agree that the more pertinent and relevant the content, the better the retention, despite the speed of success. However, at some point the students have to make the 'jump' to begin working with the abstract—books, worksheets, standardized tests, forms, etc. And this is usually where my students start having serious problems."

Lisa Gonzalves—personal communication, February 4, 2010

In this chapter we introduce a framework to follow that helps teachers such as Ms. Gonzalves guide their learners in making the "jump."

Intercultural Communication Framework

Chapter 1 explored the different ways of learning and introduced the Ways of Learning Continuum. As discussed, struggling L2 learners whose starting point is closer to the left end of the continuum frequently encounter cultural dissonance as they experience learning in their new, Western-style formal educational classroom setting.

To guide teachers in navigating this cultural divide, we propose the Intercultural Communication Framework (ICF) originally developed by Marshall (1994) from her own need as ESL teacher and teacher trainer to find effective ways of working with students from oral cultures. The premise of this framework is that when working with such L2 learners, educators must transition them to this new setting through communication that facilitates moving them from their familiar way of learning to the new way.

The ICF consists of three principles: (1) establishing and maintaining a relationship; (2) identifying and accommodating priorities; and (3) making associations between the familiar and the unfamiliar. It posits that effective communication between teachers using a Western-style model of education and students from traditional oral cultures requires careful attention to cultural factors by providing cultural scaffolding (Gay, 2002).

Forming Relationships

While a positive classroom climate promotes learning for all students, this is especially true for struggling L2 learners who thrive on a strong relationship with their teachers (Khan, 2011). Furthermore, because in many cultures teachers occupy a revered position, their role in the lives of these learners is highly important (DeCapua & Wintergerst, 2004; Lu & Bodur, 2011). Through immigration, the equilibrium of their cultural community has been disrupted, and they need to re-stabilize and rebuild their support systems. While much of their support will come from members of their own families and cultural groups, they must invariably come in contact with new support systems as well, which includes developing relationships with their teachers. However, the nature of this relationship differs from that normally existing between student and teacher in classrooms that are part of Western-style formal educational settings. Inherent in this relationship for students is an understanding of who their teachers are as people, not merely who they are in their role of teacher: Are they married, do they have children, with whom do they live? Such personal information helps these learners locate their teachers within their web of relationships. Personal connections are generally not viewed as pertinent or important to learning in Western-style, formal classrooms. In formal education, personal and professional roles and responsibilities tend to be highly compartmentalized, which can appear rigid and alienating to learners from a different cultural worldview.

The following example demonstrates this resistance to compartmentalized roles and relationships. Mrs. Horwitz, an ESL teacher, found an envelope on her desk addressed to her school with "ATTEN: Mrs. Horwitz" on it. When she opened it, she found a check and a transcript request form from a student she had had in her ESL class a few years before. Why had she, not the registrar's office, received this? Why had the student not contacted the office himself? Because Mrs. Horwitz and the student had had a relationship, he knew that she would handle it. This was not laziness or incompetence on the part of the student, but reflective of a common coping strategy in collectivistic cultures in which one person is selected or designated as the generalized contact. In more individualistic cultures, people are accustomed to dealing with people whom they do not know very well—or even at all—but in collectivistic cultures, people who do important things for each other know each other as people or know someone who knows someone (Spring, 2008; Triandis, 1995). This "someone" is a known entity in the community who commands the respect of others, whether by virtue of age, social, familial, and/or occupational status and role. Relationships are everything (Triandis, 1995).

This concept of the web of relationships extends to home-school communication. When educational institutions communicate essential information to students and their families, it is based on the assumption that the recipients will understand and respond to this communication as needed. This one-way communication often does not produce the intended result with this population because it lacks interactive elements that foster relationships and strengthen the school community web. School-to-family communication does not acknowledge that these learners and their families are looking to form webs in their lives, weaving threads among the people they meet and interact with so that a community emerges.

An analogous concept in individualistic cultures is that of "networking." However, networking implies a specific, targeted effort to create connections while for members of collectivistic cultures, communication webs are normal and expected. As the web forms from all the individuals weaving their threads to spin the web of communication, the individual threads become stronger. It is the web itself that helps to move the entire group as one, so that when one learner gains insight, that insight becomes a group insight. Therefore, instructors must create, see, strengthen, and use the invisible threads in the classroom. It is not only a social network, but also a learning network that provides support.

There is a caveat with this principle of establishing and maintaining relationships. In some instances, teachers encounter ethnic conflicts between students, who as a result, refuse to work with each other. They may bring these conflicts with them from their countries of origin or the animosity may have emerged in their new cultural contexts. Teachers and administrators need to understand the source of these conflicts and work together with the students to create a climate of respect and tolerance. The classroom must be a safe, comfortable learning web of relationships.

Identifying Priorities

Just as the teacher must take the initiative with respect to the web of relationships and communication, the teacher will also need to attend to identifying priorities. As we saw with our discussion of differing assumptions between teachers and struggling L2 learners, teachers cannot assume that these students will notice and pay attention to whatever teachers believe important. Teachers need to specify educational priorities; in order to do so, they must first examine their own assumptions and priorities. Background knowledge affects what we remember because priorities influence what we pay attention to. Spillich (1979) conducted a study comparing knowledge recall of a half inning of baseball between a group of fanatical baseball fans and a group of casual baseball fans. Results indicated that the fanatics remembered everything in great detail, with a heavy emphasis on important game-related actions. The other group recalled far fewer important details and included superficial and tangential information, such as the weather. Because the casual fans had different priorities or different internal representations of baseball, they didn't know what was and was not important with respect to the sporting event itself.

Another example of differing priorities and focus is the concept of categorization, intrinsic to Western-style formal education and based on scientific reasoning and logic (Flynn, 2007). Beginning in the earliest school years, children learn how to categorize things based on abstract, rather than on functional, characteristics. Differently colored forms are sorted according to shape, not color, so that all rectangles fit in one box, all circles in another, and so on, regardless of what colors they are. From a pragmatic perspective, color may be salient, not form. For example, weavers, potters, tailors, and other craftspeople and artisans focus on colors and how they fit together, how they affect the senses. For them, colors may well be a priority, so they will have no difficulties sorting by color but will struggle when asked to sort by shape. This is not to say that they do not recognize geometric shapes; indeed weavers, builders, and the like incorporate and make use of such shapes, but they do not categorize them abstractly. And, when they do categorize, they do so from a functional perspective, such as color, use, place in the environment, and so on. Utilitarian categorization, not scientific categorization, is their priority.

Again, from the formal perspective, the world is categorized into mammals, fish, reptiles, and the like, based on scientific classifications rather than utilitarian ones. A whale, which lives in the water, looks and acts more like a fish, yet belongs in the category "mammal" because of the characteristics "breathes air" and "nurses young that are born live." For learners coming from the left end of the Ways of Learning Continuum, it makes sense to classify whales as fish because for all intents and purposes, whales function like fish. In fact, until relatively recently with the advent and spread of scientific research and classification, whales were commonly considered fish.

The notion of priorities extends to literacy. Teachers need to keep in mind that for these students, literacy has not been essential to their lives. For them, literacy may have been limited or even non-existent or used for very specific purposes. It has not been a priority in the way that literacy is in the Western-style model of education. It is essential to note here that the focus of much pedagogy for struggling L2 learners has been the teaching of basic literacy skills. This is no doubt the key starting point in skill development; however, even with the mastery of literacy skills sufficient to function effectively in the classroom, those closer to the left side of the Ways of Learning Continuum will choose oral interaction and oral transmission over the written word because they do not make literacy a priority. In industrialized societies, lack of literacy and reliance on oral interactions in educational settings are viewed as shortcomings for which such students are penalized. They are viewed as unmotivated and unengaged when they resist the transition to reliance on print in favor of their familiar oral mode of learning.

Identifying the priorities for both the teacher and the learners is only the first step in this principle of the ICF. For any differing priority, it is up to teachers to make a decision about how to handle the resulting conflict. In accordance with the ICF, teachers need to accommodate learner priorities where possible, so as to help struggling learners feel more at home in the classroom setting. For example, when they express the need to spend time off-task getting to know their teachers better and telling their teachers more about themselves and their families, the teachers can honor that need. On the other hand, when teachers recognize a priority that will result in lack of success in the classroom, it is essential to assist the learners to yield in favor of a new perspective. Literacy, as discussed, is such a case. Academic thinking, which is based on essential precepts of formal education, is another such example. Learners in formal educational settings cannot persist in engaging only in pragmatic thinking and must make the transition to academic ways of thinking if they are to be successful in school. Even those learners who are in classes only intending to study their new language for personal reasons need to make this transition so that they can access the language, behaviors, and tasks of the classroom.

In realizing this principle, the teacher will need to observe and learn about students' priorities and then manage the accommodating and adapting process. This leads us to the third principle of the ICF.

Making Associations

The third and final principle of the framework deals with those priorities that the teacher believes are essential. The way to transition L2 learners to new priorities is by making these accessible and meaningful. Following the ICF, the most effective way to accomplish this is to understand and use familiar material and concepts from the learners' backgrounds and explicitly relate those familiar aspects to something that is new and unfamiliar to them. This type of transition is commonly discussed in the literature on reaching culturally diverse learners. For example, the "funds of knowledge" approach (González, Moll, & Amanti, 2005) takes this point of view and demonstrates how students respond more to teachers who leverage cultural backgrounds and value the knowledge students bring with them, even when this knowledge may not correspond directly to required curriculum. Furthermore, additional research on transfer of skills indicates that if a culturally different learner has acquired a skill, such as multiplication, in another setting, that skill will transfer to the new setting (Sousa, 2012).

Making associations between the known and the new is clearly a widely used and highly regarded approach. This same approach needs to be commandeered in service of new ways to access information, interact with it, demonstrate mastery of it, and then share that mastery—that is, how to "do school." The next example shows how a teacher scaffolds a new school behavior.

In Ms. Lee's class, she was working on comparing and contrasting different stores in the community. To initiate practicing this academic way of thinking, Ms. Lee began by finding out which stores the students already knew and patronized since using locations familiar to them would make it easier to teach the concept of comparing and contrasting based on store types and general products sold. The problem Ms. Lee encountered was that she asked the class who went to Wal-Mart® and no one responded. She knew (1) that they understood the question because she had been teaching them for several months and (2) that some of them shopped at Wal-Mart because it had come up in previous classes. She expected them to individually raise their hands to indicate through that gesture that they had been to that particular store. Instead, they just sat there as she repeated her question in several different ways. The change came when she went over to one student and asked him, "Do you go to Wal-Mart?" and to which he responded with an emphatic yes. She continued to go around the room, asking each student one by one the same question and receiving a response. She concluded this part of the lesson with, "If I ask the whole class, 'Who goes to Wal-Mart?' you raise your hand to answer 'yes' if it's true for you."

What was the challenge that Ms. Lee had to confront in setting this seemingly simple task? First, the students did not understand that raising their hands was part of classroom question-answer behavior. The individual hand raise was a new concept. Second, these students also did not understand the concept of providing their own response to a question asked of them by a teacher. The task was meaningless to them until Ms. Lee scaffolded it for them.

The students needed to understand this new behavior, incorporate it into this and into similar situations, and recognize the importance of this behavior in reaching their learning goals. Teachers prioritize expected classroom routines; when students fail to engage in these, such as raising one's hand to respond, teachers regard it as an unwillingness or inability on the part of students. Students' lack of participation in appropriate classroom routines and behaviors can lead teachers to labeling these students as *at risk* or *struggling* (McVee, Dunsmore, & Gavelek, 2005). In this case, that would not be correct. Instead, their difficulty stems from what we refer to here as initial contact with a new *schema*. Western-style formal education requires a multitude of new schemata, many of which are learned in the first years of schooling. If, as is the case for struggling adolescent and adult L2 learners closer to the left end of the Ways of Learning Continuum, they have not acquired these schemata in early primary years, they need to acquire them to participate actively and successfully in formal education.

In understanding this third principle of the ICF, the perspective of schema theory is useful as it permits focusing attention on the underlying assumptions and priorities that are frequently below the level of conscious awareness. In the literature, schema theory has been applied to L2 learners primarily with respect to reading comprehension, particularly the ways in which background knowledge and familiarity with the structure of texts influences their reading comprehension (e.g., Carrell, Devine, & Eskey, 1988; Roller & Matambo, 1992.) In the ICF, we approach schemata from a socio-cultural perspective highlighting the centricity of the role of culture in cognition; knowledge and people cannot be viewed as independent of each another (McVee, Dunsmore, & Gavelek, 2005). Ways of learning have cognitive consequences in the brain; mental structures—

schemata—are formed based on the patterns of understanding that have developed as a result of the types of sociocultural interactions, including those related to schooling, in which members of a given group engage (Cole, 2005; McVee, Dunsmore, & Gavelek, 2005). Thus, struggling L2 learners on the left side of the Ways of Learning Continuum will interpret and understand classroom interactions in different ways than learners accustomed to these types of interactions.

Using the three principles of the ICF, teachers culturally scaffold a new pathway for struggling L2 learners. Rather than either diluting material or presenting students with ever more information in different ways, the teacher provides a means to access and process the information by relating the unfamiliar to the familiar. We outline now how teachers can apply the ICF to the classroom. In order to do so, teachers will (1) become aware of and understand what educators' own assumptions and priorities are, (2) examine how these can be scaffolded for these students, and (3) consider what familiar material to access in service of the new concepts and new knowledge.

Applying the ICF to the Classroom

Becoming Aware of Assumptions and Priorities

Many schemata of Western-style formal education are so ingrained that educators are unaware of them. These can range from simple school routines like the individual hand raise to ways of viewing and interpreting the world. One way to identify the unfamiliar schemata is to wait for a problem to arise like Ms. Lee encountered in her lesson and, based on an understanding of the Ways of Learning Continuum and cultural differences, consider why the problem may have arisen. Another technique is to critically assess one's own teaching closely, perhaps with a colleague as an observer, and explore what is considered an essential priority that seems unfamiliar or that does not seem to be engaging the learners. Likewise, such an assessment can reveal which behaviors the students engage in that run counter to one's own expectations. The literature on schema theory indicates that many of our schemata are socio-culturally formed, often at an early age (Kozulin et al., 2003), which is consistent with our examination of culture and learning. The development of new schemata, even with a caring teacher guided by the ICF, can require considerable effort; however, the key is to provide the needed scaffolding.

Scaffolding Learning

Incremental steps are essential to transitioning struggling adolescent and adult L2 learners from their ways of learning to formal Western-style education. This requires breaking down a schema into essential parts, just as Ms. Lee did in her room. While a schema may appear incapable of being viewed as having stages or parts, it usually can be so viewed if one imagines learning it as a young child. This is what is often such a challenge for teachers of struggling adult and adolescent L2 learners—they are not children, but adolescents and adults who have yet to learn school schemata that others have acquired as part of the process of participating in Western-style formal education from a young age. And, to do so, educators must recognize that this process is *not remedial* but essential foundational instruction.

In a secondary school, Mrs. Singh, who had a primary school background, was teaching her struggling adolescent L2 learners using many of the same types of activities and tasks that she had used when she taught early grades. Because the administration did not understand the need for the ICF with this population, Mrs. Singh was viewed as "dumbing down" the curriculum and was dismissed. In fact, teachers like Mrs. Singh may be among the strongest for this population as long as they treat them age appropriately—that is, engage students in the same types of activities and tasks as they would for younger learners but use age-appropriate materials. The reason is that teachers trained to teach young children have become quite skilled in breaking down basic school schemata. Teachers of adolescents and adults may be skilled in breaking down and scaffolding complex language and concepts but not necessarily the basics of classroom interactions and tasks because they expect age-appropriate classroom schemata (DeCapua & Marshall, 2011; DeCapua, Smathers, & Tang, 2009).

Relating the New to the Familiar Material

In her lesson, Ms. Lee chose Wal-Mart because the store was down the street from the school, was very big, carried everything, and was not exclusive or expensive. She also had heard some students talking about something they had purchased there. These two methods—using what is nearby in the community and listening intently to students as they talk with each other—are both useful means of obtaining information on what is likely to be familiar to most of the students in the class. However, other means are also available and necessary.

An obvious but definitely helpful way to acquire cultural knowledge is through research on and reading about the target population. While this is important to gain insights into the students, it may or may not yield the types of underlying concepts on ways of learning necessary for a teacher trying to build new associations to foster learning in a formal educational setting. A more fruitful way to gather knowledge that is powerful culturally is to develop relationships with "cultural brokers." Cultural brokers are people who act as informants between people of different cultures (Jezewski & Sotnick, 2001). These are highly educated bilingual/bicultural people, often education professionals themselves, who have made the transition and have the knowledge of what connections can be made. For example, María, a native speaker of both Quechua and Spanish and fluent in English, is a college-educated trilingual and a parent of one of Ms. Siegal's students. She helped Ms. Siegal understand the notion that in some cultures all living objects have voice. Thus, it is not only with people that one can have conversations, but also with trees and flowers, things which most Western cultures regard as inanimate and hence "voiceless." Ms. Siegal was able to build on this knowledge when she was teaching a poem with personification. While her students already had this concept, they would not have been able to access it within an academic, literary analysis perspective if Ms. Siegal had not conferred first with María, her cultural broker.

The use of cultural brokers is consistent with the funds-of-knowledge approach that stresses the importance of understanding and incorporating the knowledge and expertise of the families of students (González, Moll, & Amanti, 2005). In the ICF, educators use cultural brokers to help them make associations between the curriculum and concepts familiar to their struggling L2 learners. Cultural brokers act as more than information sources; they are also bridges between cultures.

At Wilson High School, for example, there had been numerous incidents involving students of diverse ethnic and racial backgrounds. The administration was at a loss as to how to handle the increasingly tense and volatile situations until one teacher was able to make contact with a community person. This person was himself an immigrant from the same region as many of the students involved in the incidents and spoke several of their languages and dialects. As a cultural broker, he was able to explain the reasons for the culture clashes to the administration and the students and explore culturally sensitive ways to diffuse the tensions.

Once the teacher has established and maintained a strong ongoing two-way relationship and has identified and accommodated learner priorities insofar as possible, then the final principle of the ICF can occur. This principle is to assist struggling L2 learners in making the transition from the familiar to the unfamiliar by acting as mediating agents to facilitate the acquisition of knowledge and language within new contexts and practices.

One concrete illustration will clarify this guiding principle. For any reader of this book, a globe will be a familiar image and one that everyone immediately recognizes as representing the earth. For students new to formal educational settings, however, this may not be the case. They may not have seen globes or maps. For them, there is no basis for grasping the concept of the globe as the earth. This is true for many of the materials, concepts, and much of the knowledge teachers assume adolescent and adult learners will be familiar with, yet it is very difficult for them to see these visual representations as symbols of the concrete world they are familiar with. By showing such learners this representation of the world and then the globe itself, the teacher makes the unfamiliar become familiar. This transition to understanding representations can be viewed as moving from a three-dimensional view to a two-dimensional one. One teacher using this approach recounts this story:

> I have been teaching globes and maps to eighty mostly Karen [Burmese] newcomers this semester and trying to bridge the gap. I want to share that the issue has turned into getting them to grasp the concept of *model* and *picture*. A globe is a model of the earth; a map is a picture of the earth. So the pedagogical scaffolding has been all about providing different examples of models and pictures, starting with things they are very familiar with, and exploring how models and pictures "show" something but are not that "thing." So I have used grapefruits as models of the earth with little drawn continents on them, and then peeled them to show how the peel can be a flat "picture" of the earth, demonstrating also the distortion of a flat map, which is such a difficult concept to grasp.

It is essential for effective teaching and learning to make associations between the familiar—what students know from their informal learning and experience with the world—with the unfamiliar—school knowledge and literacy practices. There are direct conflicts between the familiar ways of learning and those expected in their new setting. However, rather than simply demand that they shift their paradigm, neither a realistic nor a particularly humane approach, teachers can ease the transition by linking the new ways of learning to familiar content and using familiar language in introducing them. To best do this, teachers need to learn about the cultures and languages of their students to make these associations explicit and utilize community resources whenever possible. In teaching a unit on health, teachers could bring in a practitioner of traditional medicine to examine such practices in conjunction with an academic science-based approach to medicine. We see a similar pattern in work that has emerged from health workers operating in developing areas of the world. Information about reproduction for low-educated rural Zimbabwean women, for example, has been shown to be much more effective if it is presented based on body maps and diagrams drawn by the people for whom it is intended rather than when presented based on Western medical models of reproductive anatomy (Cornwall, 1992). Returning to the classroom, we see that teachers need to focus on this third priority, making the transition from the familiar to the unfamiliar via creating associations. Following this principle will not only allow students to feel more at home in the classroom, it will lead struggling L2 learners to higher academic achievement.

In sum, it is the three principles of the ICF taken together that form the basis of effective interaction with struggling L2 learners, both in the society at large, and specifically, as is our concern here, in the classroom. The ICF is, in turn, the framework that underlies the instructional model presented in the next chapter.

3

Overview of MALP

Chapter 1 discussed and analyzed culturally based assumptions about learning to highlight how Western-style formal educational settings create cultural dissonance for many L2 learners who struggle in the classroom. An understanding of the Ways of Learning Continuum and the place such learners occupy on that continuum prepares educators to consider how better to instruct them. Chapter 2 presented the ICF, which established three principles for teachers to follow in conceptualizing their approach to working with students experiencing this type of cultural dissonance. This chapter combines these cultural perspectives and brings them to bear on the creation of our instructional model that addresses cultural dissonance for struggling L2 learners: the Mutually Adaptive Learning Paradigm, or MALP.

To support struggling L2 learners in their movement along the continuum from oral transmission and informal learning toward Western-style formal schooling and literacy, we have proposed MALP in several articles (DeCapua & Marshall 2010a, 2010b; Marshall & DeCapua, 2010) and in our previous book (DeCapua & Marshall, 2011). In these publications, we focused on the far end of the continuum—that is, on L2 learners from strongly collectivistic oral cultures who have had limited contact with formal education and literacy. We refer to this population as Students with Limited or Interrupted Formal Education (SLIFE). Here we expand MALP to include other L2 learners farther along on the continuum of ways of learning but still on the left, the informal learning side. As discussed in Chapter 1, such learners also struggle, with much of their difficulties rooted in cultural dissonance, albeit less strikingly than for the SLIFE subgroup. We propose that these students can benefit from MALP as they seek to achieve in classroom settings based on assumptions they only partially share. We begin by examining their learning paradigm and then considering the ways in which it also applies to those along each of the two continua examined in Chapter 1—ways of learning and collectivism-individualism.

The Learning Paradigm for SLIFE

The combination of collectivism, informal learning, and oral transmission can be viewed as a learning paradigm that contrasts with the individualistic, formal educational, literacy-based paradigm SLIFE face in the L2 classroom. Interconnectedness and shared responsibility, immediate relevance and pragmatic tasks, and oral transmission can be seen to come together to form a learning paradigm of SLIFE. We can group them into three larger categories, which constitute the components of MALP. These are: *conditions* for learning, *processes* for learning, and *activities* for learning, as shown in Figure 3.1.

FIGURE 3.1 SLIFE Learning Paradigm

SLIFE Learning Paradigm	
Component of Learning	**Element of Paradigm**
Conditions	Immediate Relevance
	Interconnectedness
Processes	Shared Responsibility
	Oral Transmission
Activities	Pragmatic Tasks

Adapted from DeCapua & Marshall, 2011.

Learning Paradigm for Struggling L2 Learners

We now reexamine this paradigm in light of those learners who are not SLIFE but who also experience extensive cultural dissonance. These struggling L2 learners continue to experience difficulties with the demands of the classroom, rooted as they are in the individualistic, academic, literacy-focused world in which they find themselves as participants.

Conditions for Learning

Mr. Morris has just been introduced to his new class. The previous teacher is on leave and may or may not return. The students liked their previous teacher but now need to adjust to Mr. Morris. After he had been introduced by the director of the program, one of the students asked, "You marry?" after which another student immediately chimed in with, "You have how many child?" As he answered the questions, he showed the class two photos he had with him of his family, telling the students who everyone was and their ages. Mr. Morris began to establish a relationship with the students as he asked them the same questions and everyone learned more about each other's families.

In the MALP framework, we understand that for learning to take place, there are conditions a learner requires and/or prefers. Although these may differ from person to person, there are some culturally based conditions for learning that underlie the experience. First, those students need to feel part of an interconnected group of learners and teachers, given their predominantly collectivistic cultural orientations. Second, they need to believe that what they are learning will be immediately relevant to their lives outside of the classroom as a result of their utilitarian perspective. To illustrate the notion of interconnectedness, consider Mr. Morris's actions—Mr. Morris used personal photos as a means to build interconnectedness. For these learners, it is essential to know the teacher in order to learn from him, and Mr. Morris has set the stage for their learning. And, by discussing his family and theirs, Mr. Morris is using a topic of immediate relevance to them.

Thus, the learning paradigm of these students includes two conditions for learning—*interconnectedness* and *immediate relevance*. As long as they feel that these two conditions are present, they are likely to become more comfortable in a Western-style formal educational setting than when there is no such connection or relevance.

Processes for Learning

The next component of the learning paradigm includes the processes through which learners prefer to assimilate new material and build skills and knowledge. Processes are the ways in which learners prefer to receive new material for learning and how they expect to interact with that material. These processes for learning, like the conditions for learning, derive from culturally based mores. If we closely revisit assumptions about learning, we find that two of them describe processes for learning these students use to internalize new material: (1) the expectation that learners share knowledge, skills, and understanding with each other and support each other as they learn; and (2) the belief that through oral interaction with each other and their teacher, they will master the lesson. Thus, their learning paradigm includes two processes for learning: *shared responsibility,* again drawn from their generally collectivistic cultural orientation, and *oral transmission*, resulting from their experience with and preference for orality. Orality is a way of life for them that goes beyond foreign and second language classroom notions of oral proficiency. The sharing of responsibility derives from their feelings of interconnectedness and becomes a process on which they draw in their learning. Relying on their oral communicative style and preferences as a process is essential for them as they are new to literacy. They will feel familiar and comfortable in classrooms that incorporate both processes: shared responsibility and orality.

Let us return to Mr. Morris.

After discussing the photos and families in this first lesson, Mr. Morris asks the students to tell him what they were learning with the other teacher. He has received some paperwork that orients him, but he would like to see what the students can tell him about their studies. In addition, he wants to give them the opportunity to practice through the oral mode. Finally, he welcomes the opportunity to put them in the role of informing him, so that he becomes the learner. He writes what they tell him on the board, with the students jumping in to add their ideas about what they have been studying, while Mr. Morris asks questions or adds something along the way. At the end, the class has produced a list for him and a review for themselves.

Activities for Learning

The third component of a learning paradigm includes the activities that teachers design for their students. As we have seen, struggling L2 learners are more accustomed to utilitarian tasks than decontextualized ones. Knowing this, Mr. Morris sets up an activity for learning that requires students to perform familiar experience-based tasks.

To prepare the students for a homework assignment and the next lesson, Mr. Morris asks the students to brainstorm a list of what family members do and writes their ideas on the board. For homework, he tells them to choose one of the items, take a photo of a family member doing it, and bring it to class. In the subsequent class, the students put their photos together and make a collage.

Through this activity, the students are making a home-to-school connection and are engaging in a meaningful, relevant group project. Their work results in a display illustrating the lifestyles of their families. This type of activity conforms to the expectations of struggling L2 learners, giving them an opportunity to demonstrate their understanding of the task in a concrete, accessible manner—namely, a class collage.

By the end of the week, the students feel comfortable with Mr. Morris because he has been teaching using the the Learning Paradigm shown in Figure 3.1.

Western-Style Learning Paradigm

These same students also have a class with Mrs. Shim, a very different type of teacher. We now turn to Mrs. Shim's science class.

> The class is learning about the microscope. Mrs. Shim begins by asking the students for the definition of a microscope. Because they are not sure, she writes a definition on the board and asks them to copy it into their notebooks. Then Mrs. Shim asks them why scientists use microscopes and how they are different from telescopes. When she is answered by silence, she explains it to them and asks them to take notes on her answers. Next, Mrs. Shim teaches them the parts of the microscope using a diagram and a vocabulary list. They have a worksheet with a diagram of the microscope with lines pointing to the various parts and blank lines on which to write the correct words. In their workbook, there is a vocabulary list of microscope parts and Mrs. Shim asks the students to label the microscope by selecting and then copying the vocabulary into the numbered blanks around the diagram. She calls on each student one at a time to give the correct response. She ends by telling them to study their notes about the microscope and vocabulary on the diagram and to prepare for a quiz the next day on the microscope. By the end of the week, the students feel anxious and are worried that they will not be able to learn from her.

Mrs. Shim is teaching through the lens of Western-style formal education with its conditions, processes, and activities, as shown in Figure 3.2.

FIGURE 3.2 Western-Style Formal Education Paradigm

Western-Style Formal Education Paradigm	
Component of Learning	**Element of Paradigm**
Conditions	Future Relevance
	Independence
Processes	Individual Accountability
	Written Word
Activities	Decontextualized Tasks

Adapted from DeCapua & Marshall, 2011.

As most readers are likely to teach following the Western-style formal education paradigm, these elements may seem quite familiar and unremarkable. But what may immediately strike a reader in looking at this learning paradigm is how it directly contrasts with the learning paradigm of struggling L2 learners. We particularly draw attention to activities for learning and decontextualized tasks.

Mrs. Shim expects her students to provide a definition when asked and that it be based on a scientific analysis with characteristics that describe the term. So, when she asks for a definition of *lens*, for example, she does not expect students to say merely, "something for seeing small things." Similarly, with categorization, Mrs. Shim looks for students to see parts of words, such as prefixes, roots, and suffixes (*micro* = "small," *scope* = "look," and so on.), but her class of struggling L2 learners will more likely just try and take the first, middle, and last letters arbitrarily if they try at all to comply with her request to divide a word into parts. In this lesson, knowing the importance of academic language and content concepts, she is requiring her students to define, categorize, and demonstrate their ability to engage in thinking derived from the tenets of formal education. In subsequent lessons, Mrs. Shim, familiar with Bloom's taxonomy, challenges the students to move from the lower- to higher-order thinking skills and makes these a priority in her classroom.

Teachers like Mrs. Shim who follow a Western-style formal education paradigm are trying to help students succeed through a new way of learning. However, in Mrs. Shim's class, the learners are being required to make a complete paradigm shift, which is extremely difficult for them given the total newness of its elements—the assumptions of Western-style formal education. In contrast, teachers like Mr. Morris follow their students' paradigm to make the students feel comfortable and match their expectations for learning. In his class, the students are not held individually accountable, interaction is nearly exclusively oral, and the activity does not build the skills valued in the classroom. Here we have two approaches to working with struggling L2 learners, neither of which appears to be an appropriate solution to the lack of success.

Reconciling the Paradigms—MALP

How then do we reconcile these two contrasting paradigms? The instructional model proposed in this book comes from a mutually adaptive perspective. We take an approach that combines the two paradigms for learning and views struggling L2 learners as transitioning from one paradigm to the other. MALP does not demand that teachers completely adapt their teaching to the ways of learning of their students, nor does it attempt to replace the students' familiar ways with those of the Western-style paradigm. Instead, MALP allows for a blending of the two paradigms, supporting learners as they move from familiar to unfamiliar and maintaining selected aspects of the learner's paradigm throughout. The result is a new, mutually adaptive paradigm that takes into account both perspectives, those of struggling L2 learners and those of the formal educational setting.

Figure 3.3 shows MALP and how it draws elements from each of the two paradigms. In the left-hand column are the three components of MALP:

1. accept the conditions from struggling L2 learners

2. combine processes from struggling L2 learners and Western-style education

3. focus on Western-style activities but use familiar language and content.

The other two columns show the two learning paradigms—that of struggling L2 learners and that of Western-style education. The elements of MALP, drawn from both paradigms, are bolded and shaded. They are:

1. learner conditions: **immediate relevance** and **interconnectedness**

2. combined processes of learners and Western-style education: **shared responsibility** and **individual accountability** together with **oral transmission** and the **written word**

3. Western-style learning activities: **decontextualized tasks** scaffolded by familiar language and content.

FIGURE 3.3 Mutually Adaptive Learning Paradigm (MALP)

Components of Learning	Struggling L2 Learners	Western-Style Education
ACCEPT CONDITIONS from learners.	Immediate Relevance	Future Relevence
	Interconnectedness	Independence
COMBINE PROCESSES from learners and Western-style education	Shared Responsibility	Individual Accountability
	Oral Transmission	Written Word
FOCUS on Western-style learning ACTIVITIES with familiar language and content	Pragmatic Tasks	Decontextualized Tasks

Because future relevance, independence, and pragmatic tasks are not elements of MALP, they remain unbolded and unshaded.

Taken together, these elements form a new paradigm, one that teachers can use to bridge the cultural dissonance and transition struggling L2 learners to their new classroom setting.

Conditions for Learning in MALP

What are the priorities of each paradigm that can be incorporated into learning? How can these be accommodated in the classroom to transition struggling L2 learners to Western-style formal education? In MALP, teachers accommodate the conditions for learning that are most important for these students—interconnectedness and immediate relevance. As we have seen, collectivistic learners seek not to distinguish themselves as independent individuals but prefer to form a network, a web that interconnects them with each other. This preference for interconnectedness extends to their learning. A sense of shared responsibility flows from that, so that they will look to each other for support as they complete learning activities in the classroom (Gay, 2000). Similarly, as students experienced with informal ways of learning have a cultural priority to seek immediate relevance in their endeavors and are not focused on future relevance, they need to find such relevance in the classroom. Immediate relevance is based on the primacy of pragmatic tasks in their lives. Teachers in Western-style educational settings frequently believe that they are seeking to make connections with students and to make their work with their students relevant to their lives; however, the extent to which this is a priority differs greatly for them and for their struggling L2 learners who see immediate relevance in terms of pragmatic tasks and knowledge (Gutiérrez, 2008; Gutiérrez, Baquedano-Lopez, & Tejada, 1999). Learning about animal husbandry, how to enact specific religious practices, or engaging in household chores have concrete and visible results and are tied to their immediate experiences. A focus on the future—a time when the learner will function independently of the teacher and when the learning will bear fruit—characterizes Western-style schooling. Moreover, much of what is learned is not as important as developing abilities, such as learning different ways of thinking (Ozmon & Carver, 2008).

Processes for Learning in MALP

With respect to literacy, struggling L2 learners with no or limited literacy favor oral transmission as the primary mode for learning and do not regard the written word as a meaningful way for them to access new ideas or gain knowledge, either in their first or their second language. Even for those struggling L2 learners who have literacy skills, it is a matter of their preference for oral transmission over print. In Western-style formal education, literacy is paramount and without it, success is impossible. In addition, students must demonstrate learning, not as part of a group, but as individuals. Expecting struggling L2 learners to acquire and demonstrate their learning as independent individuals through the written word exacerbates their cultural dissonance. Since this instructional model is mutually adaptive, teachers incorporate learners' traditions of shared responsibility and oral transmission as they transition them to literacy and individual responsibility and accountability. The principle of moving from familiar to unfamiliar underlies the combining of processes for learning. In MALP, the teacher encourages struggling L2 learners to rely in part on their preference for sharing the learning as a group and for using their oral traditions to internalize what they are learning, while at the same time introducing them to new processes. Without grounding in their own familiar processes for learning, these learners can become lost and overwhelmed (Marshall, DeCapua, & Antolini, 2010).

Activities for Learning in MALP

Struggling L2 learners must master decontextualized tasks in order to demonstrate learning in a way that is recognized in formal education, whether K-12, adult education, or work-based. Students cannot succeed with only pragmatic ways of thinking as they were doing in Mr. Morris' class. The tasks they will now engage in require the development of new schemata. The ways of thinking embodied in decontextualized tasks are a priority that must be addressed. If we refer back to Bloom's taxonomy (Bloom 1956; revised Anderson & Krathwohl, 2001), we see that it is a systematic classification of thinking and learning governing essential criteria of Western-style formal education. As they select activities for their lessons, teachers focus on decontextualized tasks that exemplify one or more of these processes.

An activity for learning includes a task, but the task in and of itself does not constitute a learning activity. There are two other aspects to each learning activity that accompany the task. In order to be a learning activity, a task needs to be based on content from a curriculum, syllabus, or other source, which provides a new content schema. In addition, the task needs to be in the language of instruction. In the case of L2 students, because their native languages differ from the language of instruction, the linguistic schema is new. The task set by the teacher, representing the formal schema for the activity, will likely embody academic ways of thinking. For struggling L2 learners, these too will be largely unfamiliar and demanding. Thus, all three aspects of a learning activity are new and unfamiliar to struggling L2 the learners.

The most common assumption is that students' primary difficulty is the language or content when, in fact, *it is the task itself that may be causing the major barrier.* To assess what is causing this barrier to learning, teachers need to break down the process into incremental steps so that students move from a completely new task to one they can complete without disorientation. Doing so helps teachers establish that it is not the task that is causing the difficulty. Teachers need to shift their own thinking so that they regard learning through these new activities as building the new schemata discussed in Chapter 2. Learning can be overwhelming for struggling L2 learners if there are too many new schemata. Once the activities themselves become familiar schemata, the teacher can shift the students to academic language and/or academic content and move them through the curriculum. It is important to focus on separating and balancing the three schemata.

For example, if students are asked to tell a familiar folktale in their own language, they generally have few difficulties in doing so; on the other hand, if they are asked to summarize a paragraph in their textbook, they struggle to complete the task. What is the difference between these two activities? If these activities are viewed through the lens of schema theory, we see that classroom activities, such as the summarizing, commonly have embedded in them three schemata: linguistic, content, and formal schemata. If all three are unfamiliar—that is, if learners do not have the language, the background knowledge, or this

FIGURE 3.4 The Three Schemata

Schemata	Description	Examples
Linguistic	the language in which the activity is presented and in which the student must respond	first language; second/dialect language
Content	the subject matter the activity is asking the student to address	school subjects at grade level; basic education competencies; vocational/technical knowledge; culture-based information
Formal	the type of task that the activity requires the student to perform	assessment formats: true/false, matching, multiple choice; critical-thinking skills: defining, summarizing

decontextualized way of thinking—the task will be impossible for learners (DeCapua & Marshall, 2011). In fact, even in cases where L2 learners have progressed to a level of language proficiency that permits comprehension and, thus, presumably has the linguistic schema, such academic tasks are still very difficult. Figure 3.4 illustrates the three different schemata and provides examples.

We can clarify this more by looking at three students and tasks they have been asked to perform by their teacher, Mrs. Ortega, outlined in Figure 3.5. In Example 1, Mrs. Ortega asks José to summarize a story he knows from his culture in his native language. The only new schema is the formal schema, summarizing, because he is using his native language and a familiar story. In Example 2, Mrs. Ortega asks Omar to summarize the story the class just read in English. Here he confronts all three schemata as difficult, not only the task. In Example 3, Mrs. Ortega has Mati practice the numbers in English as vocabulary and asks

FIGURE 3.5 Mrs. Ortega's Classroom Tasks

Mrs. Ortega's Classroom Tasks			
Example	**Language (L)**	**Content (C)**	**Formal**
1 José	L1—familiar	C1—story familiar	Summarize—unfamiliar
2 Omar	L2—unfamiliar	C2—story unfamiliar	Summarize—unfamiliar
3 Mati	L2—unfamiliar	Classroom furniture— familiar	Counting practice— familiar

her to count the chairs in the classroom. Mati is focusing on the linguistic schemata because the task of counting is a practice task with which she is familiar and the "content"—the chairs in the classroom—is also familiar to her.

This third component of MALP, which requires the teacher to introduce new activities using familiar language and content, as well as balance the three schemata, is perhaps the most difficult aspect of the model to plan effectively. The teacher needs to become comfortable thinking in terms of three aspects of the activity—task + language + content—and balancing them so that the learner has some familiar aspect of the learning activity to connect with. This balancing clearly did not occur in Mrs. Shim's science classroom, where all three schemata were unfamiliar in her activities exploring the use of a microscope. The key is to continually focus on one of the three to assist the learner in completing the activity successfully. The schema that is being focused on is scaffolded so that the students increasingly gain mastery.

MALP Checklist

To help teachers implement MALP, we have developed a checklist (DeCapua & Marshall, 2011) with the elements of MALP described. The MALP Checklist, shown in Figure 3.6, guides teachers to ensure that they are implementing the instructional model. Doing so requires all six elements. If one element is left out, then the model will not be applied faithfully; the MALP Checklist helps the teacher identify specific aspects of the instruction that speak to each of the elements and add or change the plans for the lesson as needed.

In order to implement the checklist in any given class, teachers need to ask themselves three important questions:

1. What is immediately relevant for these students?
2. What is familiar content for these students?
3. What is familiar language for these students?

Without this information, the teacher will not be able to implement MALP.

Let's revisit the two classrooms discussed earlier in the chapter using the MALP Checklist. Although Mr. Morris' teaching was congruent with the learners' paradigm, from the MALP perspective, his teaching lacked essential elements. Mr. Morris included only three of the six elements of MALP: immediate relevance, interconnectedness, and use of familiar language and content. After learning about MALP and by using the MALP Checklist, Mr. Morris turned his lessons into MALP lessons for his class.

FIGURE 3.6 MALP Checklist (DeCapua & Marshall, 2011)

Mutually Adaptive Learning Paradigm – MALP
Teacher Planning Checklist

A. Accept Conditions for Learning

A1. I am making this lesson/project immediately relevant to students. ☐

A2. I am helping students develop and maintain interconnectedness. ☐

B. Combine Processes for Learning

B1. I am incorporating both shared responsibility and individual accountability. ☐

B2. I am scaffolding the written word through oral interaction. ☐

C. Focus on New Activities for Learning

C1. I am focusing on tasks requiring academic ways of thinking. ☐

C2. I am making these tasks accessible with familiar language and content. ☐

Copyright © 2013 University of Michigan. This page is reproducible.

Mr. Morris' MALP Revised Lesson

While Mr. Morris is showing his family photos and talking about his family, he writes key words and sentences on the board: *wife, son, daughter, White Plains.* To encourage literacy development via oral transmission, he points to each word and asks the students to repeat them. The students read and repeat the sentences with Mr. Morris pointing to them initially, and then different students doing so. In this way, students are becoming accustomed to making explicit associations between the oral and print modes.

After reviewing key words and phrases with the students, Mr. Morris asks if anyone has a photo to share. Melisa has a photo of herself with her four children. The class helps her describe her photo while Mr. Morris writes the information on the board.

> I have four children. I have three sons. I have one daughter. My daughter is 15 years old. My son Angel is 19 years old. My son Raimundo is 17 years old. My son Johnny is 14 years old.

When they have finished, Melisa reads as Mr. Morris points to each word. He then asks for another volunteer. Natalie stands next to Melisa and, with help from the other students, describes Melisa's photo while Mr. Morris again writes.

> Melisa has four children. She has three sons. She has one daughter. Her daughter is 15 years old. Her son Angel is 19 years old. Her son Raimundo is 17 years old. Her son Johnny is 14 years old.

The students read the story together aloud as Natalie points to each word. They then copy the second story into their notebooks.

What learners know and can talk about, they can write. What they write, they can read, and they can read what others write. Thus, the teacher can transition them to a greater level of comfort with the written word and with individual accountability, while at the same time focusing on new ways of thinking. In addition, given the importance such learners place on interconnectedness, their participation in a shared experience fosters the sense of the class and teacher as a community.

Later, when the students work on their individual collages, Mr. Morris ensures that there is both group sharing and individual responsibility. In pairs, the students prepare their collages, helping each other decide what pictures and written information to include. Individually, they are each responsible for the creation of their own personal collage. Once they have completed this step, Mr.

Morris works on developing new ways of thinking, using familiar language and content. He has each pair prepare a Venn diagram that compares and contrasts their families based on the information in their collages. He models this step by drawing a large Venn diagram on the board. He writes his name on one side and has a volunteer, Ana, come up to the front of the class with her collage. With input from the other students, Ana and Mr. Morris complete the Venn diagram, showing how their families are similar and different. He has successfully taken the class from the contextualized presentation of the personal collages into a decontextualized graphic organizer.

Mrs. Shim's MALP Revised Lesson

Mrs. Shim has the opposite problem. She is using even fewer elements of MALP. She is using only one—focus on new activities for learning—all of which are decontextualized and not scaffolded with familiar language and content. To alter her lesson on the microscope so that it would include all the elements of MALP, Mrs. Shim rethinks her lesson using the MALP Checklist.

To introduce the concept of a microscope and why we use it, Mrs. Shim brings in a variety of spices. She shows the students two or three of her favorite spices, such as salt, pepper, and cinnamon, at least some of which she thinks her students will be familiar with. She explains to the class why these spices are important to her, describes some dishes she likes to use them for, and passes samples around so that everyone can smell, touch, and even taste them. Next, Mrs. Shim has the students examine slides that she has prepared with these spices under the microscope .

After everyone has had a chance to look at the slides, she has the students tell her what they saw under the microscope versus with just their own eyes and what surprised them about seeing these same spices under the microscope. As they talk, Mrs. Shim lists and reviews with them pertinent vocabulary words on the blackboard. She also asks them to tell her their favorite spice and lists these on the board in English if they know the name in English, translated if she knows it, or in their language if they can help her write it. She then elicits from the students why they like this spice. If they mention any of the other spices she has brought in, she can also pass them around and let them look at them on slides.

For the main part of the lesson, labeling the diagram of the microscope, she introduces the students to the concept of filling in labels on a diagram by using something familiar, such as the classroom. First the class names items in the classroom, which Mrs. Shim lists on the board. Mrs. Shim then makes a diagram of the classroom and draws blank lines for about four or five of the items on the list. Together, she and the students fill in the blanks by choosing the words from the list on the board. Next, Mrs. Shim has the students, working in pairs or small groups, make their own diagrams of the classroom adding five to six blank lines for other items from the list they decide they want to include. They exchange their diagrams and fill in the blanks on the diagrams that their classmates have created. These steps scaffold the process so that struggling L2 learners understand labeling, an academic way of thinking, before they have to label the microscope. The microscope is unfamiliar in and of itself, in addition to the unfamiliar task of labeling. Because the classroom items are in their immediate environment, the labeled diagrams have relevance. Mrs. Shim created a familiar context, the classroom, and decontextualized it as a scaffold to move her students into labeling objects.

Finally, they will be better prepared for the activities with academic language and content that Mrs. Shim originally intended for them. By understanding the principles of MALP and using the MALP Checklist, Mrs. Shim finds ways to enhance her instruction and scaffold learning for her class, so they do not feel overwhelmed and their cultural dissonance is lessened.

This chapter outlined how MALP is a roadmap for teachers to follow as they journey with their classes of struggling L2 learners from informal learning to formal education. MALP is grounded in the ICF because it calls for a recognition that both paradigms are valued and important and supports the belief that a mutually adaptive approach will result in greater success for struggling L2 learners. All the elements of MALP derive from the principles of the ICF and are designed to (1) lessen cultural dissonance by providing support from familiar schemata and honoring learner priorities and (2) transition learners to the new schemata they need to master in order to succeed in school. The learner priorities that can be accommodated are incorporated into the classroom and those that cannot are transitioned into new priorities using the support of the familiar; essential processes from both their learning paradigm and the learning paradigm of formal schooling are combined. Finally, instruction is focused on new academic ways of thinking and decontextualized tasks, scaffolded by familiar language and content.

4

Scaffolding Academic Ways of Thinking and Responding

Mr. Mancuso asks the class, "What is an owl pellet?" Diego had seen owl pellets and could identify them but had never talked about them. He saw that Mr. Mancuso had placed an owl pellet on the table in front of the classroom, so he pointed to it. Mr. Mancuso turned away from Diego and asked the rest of the class again, "Who can define owl pellet?"

Diego believed that he had responded appropriately by physically identifying the object, but from Mr. Mancuso's point of view, that was not enough. Knowing what an owl pellet is and being able to provide a definition are separate abilities; and in the classroom setting "to define is to know" (DeCapua & Marshall, 2011). In fact, the most common question asked in classrooms is the one that requires the student to define: "What is X?" (Cazden, 2001). When a teacher asks this question, it is not sufficient to point or give an example; rather a student must provide salient characteristics, functions, and categories appropriate to the given term or concept. By contrast, questions that ask for explicit definitions are not common in informal settings where much of learning takes place through observing and then imitating older family or community members in the practical application of information (Paradise & Rogoff, 2009).

In this vignette, while Diego is focused on the content and his understanding of it, his teacher is focused on the academic language associated with the content and the oral participation required to demonstrate mastery of that language along with the content. This act of defining is a communication priority in formal educational settings (O'Keeffe, McCarthy, & Carter, 2007). Mr. Mancuso has neither accommodated the learner priority to demonstrate understanding

through alternate means nor helped support Diego in using the type of unfamiliar formalistic language needed to produce the expected definition of the familiar owl pellet. Until Mr. Mancuso is aware of the differences in learning
paradigms and priorities, he will not be able to address the fundamental learning issues. We cannot understand or address that of which we are unaware.

Watson (2010) describes a powerful instance of this in an anecdote from a
sheltered ESL science class for newcomers, the majority being students with limited or interrupted formal education, at a large urban high school. The students
were asked to classify activities such as hockey, bowling, tennis, swimming,
golfing, gardening, etc., according to whether they were indoor activities, out-
door activities, or both. She writes:

> The truly astounding moment came at the end of class, when the very
> kind and well-meaning teacher went through the activity with the
> class, displaying correct answers on the overhead projector, as stu-
> dents rushed to confirm and correct their responses in one of those
> flying eraser moments so common in such classes. When he got to
> tennis and asked how it should be classified, an unusual number of
> hands flew up—the students who had been bussing to an athletic club
> for months to attend tennis class were confident to say that tennis was
> an indoor activity. The teacher's answer key, though, had this listed as
> an outdoor activity, and so after some animated discussion, he finally
> decided that, "We will just *say* that it's an outdoor activity, ok?" (pp.
> 167–168)

Watson makes the point that this illustrates the ease with which the teacher and
those educated under the Western-style learning paradigm "can adopt an arm's-
length relationship to knowledge; we can just *say* that something is what it isn't
if it helps us get a good grade—it doesn't matter anyway" (p. 168). Watson continues: "Oral cultures do not think of knowledge this way. Knowledge comes
from experience, is transmitted within experiences, and always matters" (p.
168). Tasks such as classifying and defining, however, are based on academic
ways of thinking and require specific types of language. Teaching these types of
language must be preceded by instruction in the concepts that underlie such
language. Grasping the concept of defining, as well as the importance of being
able to articulate definitions, must precede setting the task itself.

To use such tasks as a starting point for instruction places unreasonable
demands on students from backgrounds where such types of thinking and language use are not normal behaviors. Struggling L2 learners need to know what

to select, how to organize information, and how to interpret the information from a Western-style learning paradigm. Often, instruction jumps to the interpretation stage as the initial focus for content learning. This population first needs to learn how to build definitions and understand why they are important. Then they need practice analyzing what to select and how to organize the information. Developing academic ways of thinking and using both oral and written language to express that type of thinking are essential to success in today's classrooms and in the workplace. (Genesee, et al., 2006; Parrish & Johnson, 2010; Roessingh, Kover, & Watt, 2005). From a historical perspective, until the latter part of the twentieth century, students were not necessarily required to demonstrate learning beyond what is now referred to as the lower-order thinking skills. At that time, many students could learn survival English, go through the educational system, and then move into manufacturing, without ever engaging in the type of oral and written discourse associated with schooling (Flynn, 2007). Today, extensive memorizing and basic survival skills will not lead to achievement in a new setting, although they may be sufficient for non-school activities. It is essential to introduce all students to academic ways of thinking for success in today's world (Reimer, 2008). This imperative includes both the adolescent and adult populations that concern us in this book.

This chapter focuses on scaffolding academic thinking and responding and places them sequentially into skill sets: higher-order thinking skills, discussion skills, writing skills, and test-taking skills. The term *academic thinking* refers to ways of viewing and organizing the world that are derived from Western-style formal education and that are grounded in the scientific tradition, as explained in Chapter 1.

Scaffolding Higher-Order Thinking Skills

As shown in the discussion of assumptions common to North American teachers and learners (see Chapter 1), it is difficult to become aware of one's expectations regarding the classroom. Similarly, it is necessary to examine assumptions about ways of thinking, such as defining. On a deeper level, teachers, like Mr. Mancuso, need to make explicit for struggling L2 learners that fundamental to academic tasks are broad categories of thought based on scientific principles.

An initial step in developing the underlying concepts is helping struggling L2 learners grasp the importance of explicitly formalizing the relationship of one idea to another. Struggling L2 learners, especially those closer to the left side of the Ways of Learning Continuum, find it more natural to think of ideas as a chain to which links are added consecutively. This is an additive approach to connecting ideas that does not make clear an underlying relationship between two ideas and presents each one in turn, leaving it to the listener to "connect the dots" (Ong, 1982). The priority for these students on the left side is remembering the ideas, bringing them to others, and keeping them alive. The energy is focused on a sequence of listening, remembering, and retelling. In formal Western-style classrooms, however, these tasks are not regarded as sufficient for scholastic achievement. Returning to the MALP instructional model, recall the importance of introducing the academic ways of thinking using familiar language and content.

In the examination of the several ways of thinking, the teachers in the examples cited are using familiar language and content as scaffolding for their instruction so that, in keeping with balancing the schemata, the formal schema—the unfamiliar way of thinking—is the sole unfamiliar schema in the lesson.

Grouping: Categorization and Classification

Understanding the formalistic organization of information is crucial for societal and scholastic success. While there are many types of organization, one of the most common is to establish categories, recognize classifications, or in some other way form conceptual groupings. Even defining presupposes, as we saw, understanding categorization because when we define, we are placing something into a broad category. Cultures conceptualize and categorize the material world differently, choosing culture-specific divisions regarding animate-inanimate, gender, colors, or divisions of time (see, e.g., Deutscher, 2010; Lakoff, 1990). Across languages and cultures, people do not see the same groupings, an issue that all L2 learners have to contend with. Popular best practices for teaching defining, such as the Frayer Model (Frayer, Frederick, & Klausmeier, 1969), may themselves be an obstacle to learning due to divergent assumptions based on classifications. In the Frayer Model, students approach the definition of a term or concept by identifying such items as typical characteristics or non-examples. In addition, the concept of having to group, by either categorizing or classifying, may be unfamiliar and thus has to be scaffolded for struggling L2 learners.

Categorizing is the sorting of phenomena into groups appropriate to a situation in order to impose order. *Classifying,* on the other hand, involves sorting phenomena into recognized, fixed classes or dividing things into groups according to their type. Bats, horses, whales, and cows are classified as mammals because they share specific characteristics, such as having live births and being warm-blooded. Categorizing is a good starting point as it is more flexible than classification.

The key to scaffolding categories is to begin with specific, personal categories that are easily accessed in the classroom. Ms. Chen, for example, went to one corner of the classroom and asked Jose to go into the other. She asked Sophia to join her in her corner, and Muhammed in José's. The class soon caught on that one corner was for boys and one for girls. This activity quickly taught the concept of sorting by gender. The next step was to sort photos of people of all ages, ethnicities, colors, and backgrounds, teaching students again to focus on only gender as a category.

Once the students have grasped the general idea of categorizing and sorting, they can be given a larger number of items. The teacher can ask the students to demonstrate different motor/motion verbs, such as *walk, run, jump,* and *hop.* Figure 4.1 illustrates how this can be done:

- The teacher gives the student a sentence such as *When we run, we use feet, hands, earth. We do not use water.*
- As she reads the sentence, she points to the verb *run* on the chart and, reading down the first column on the left, points to each noun and adds a plus or minus sign.
- The class continues completing the rest of the chart, either reading chorally or with one student taking the lead.
- They then can expand the activity by identifying the characteristics of a given verb. *Jumping,* for instance, means going up and down while *hopping* is the same, but on one foot.

By creating such a collaborative class chart, they are conducting semantic feature analysis. Semantic feature analysis can be used as a scaffolding tool for this type of thinking: Which ones do we do with two feet? Which ones are fast?

FIGURE 4.1 Semantic Feature Analysis

	run	walk	ride	swim
feet	+	+	-	+
hands	+	-	-	+
earth	+	+	+ -	-
water	-	-	+ -	+

Because the activities are familiar and can be demonstrated physically, as in Total Physical Response or TPR (Asher, 1969), the content and language are not barriers. The formal schema of categorizing is the new element here.

The next step after extracting the factors is to present them or evaluate them in a very formulaic manner. This can be a chart, table, diagram, outline, or any type of graphic organizer. It can be a specific type of document, such as a lab report or essay. It can also be the response to particular types of elicitation formats commonly used to glean the student's level of understanding of given organizational content. After engaging the class in semantic feature analysis, for example, the teacher sets up a task such as, "List two characteristics of swimming."

As we saw with Diego and the owl pellet, defining requires understanding categorization and classification. In order to define something, students have to know how it is grouped, or as stated earlier, *to define is to know.* To understand how to group something, students need to identify those characteristics, similarities, and differences that are salient from a scientific, empiricist, Western-based approach.

Comparison and Contrast

A common classroom task is to ask students to compare and contrast two items. To do this, students must demonstrate an understanding of how ideas are connected beyond the additive approach they normally use. For example, a student may state, *I like this juice and I don't like that one.* While familiar with both juices, (content schema) and able to say which one they like (linguistic schema), students would not think to compare and contrast them (formal schema) as a learning activity. Rather they would simply make them and then serve and drink them. They may comment, as this student does, that they like or do not like the taste. The student in our example was clearly expressing a contrast, despite the use of the word *and* instead of the typical words and phrases associated with comparison and contrast, such as *but*, *on the other hand*, or *in contrast*.

In a science class, if the teacher asked the students to compare two types of juice, they would be asked to look at such factors as the acidity. In these tasks, there is a specific logic that is followed in order to lay out the various factors that one is comparing and contrasting, such as taste, color, ingredients and their percentages, and so on. This logic is not based on personal experience but on scientific reasoning, the foundation of Western-style formal education. In a classroom, one is expected to extract the similarities and differences from an objective viewpoint. How, then, would we answer the question posed earlier,

"What do a dog and rabbit have in common?" Incorrect responses would be dogs make good pets but rabbits don't or my uncle has a dog to hunt rabbits because these are neither objective nor scientific (Flynn, 2007). The "correct" answer would be that they are both mammals because they are warm-blooded, have fur, give birth to live young, and nurse their young. A true definition is created by students being able to demonstrate understanding of a particular type of classification and the specific characteristics of the item being defined. Rather than create a context for the dog and the rabbit showing how they relate to each other in the real world, the classroom task is to decontextualize the two animals for the purpose of analysis.

To scaffold the juice comparison task for struggling L2 learners, the teacher can begin by asking the students to compare two types of juice based on their personal preference. They might give examples of the two juices' similarities or differences based on their own viewpoint and preferences. Mei wrote *Juice A is sweet; however, Juice B is sour.* The teacher can then have the students look at other readily visible characteristics that are similar or different, entering them in a Venn diagram, with two overlapping circles. The teacher enters on each of the non-overlapping circles differences, or unique characteristics, and similarities in the overlapping part. Fang offered, *Juice A is orange; however, Juice B is purple.* Lydia, pointing to both, said *for drink.* Mrs. Terhune entered *orange* on one side, *purple* on the other, and *for drinking* in the middle.

Once the students have understood the essentials of comparison and contrast using familiar language and content, they can perform these tasks using more complex language and more challenging content. All of these tasks demonstrate the students' understanding of the formal relationship between ideas. Academic thinking requires showing how ideas relate to each other, as comparison and contrast, which was just illustrated. Although the additive relationship is certainly one of these, teachers need to introduce alternative relationships to broaden struggling L2 learners' repertoire in demonstrating academic ways of thinking.

Scaffolding Discussion Skills

Once a particular concept, such as grouping, becomes familiar to the students, the next step is to introduce the appropriate discourse for that concept. As we continue to balance the schemata, the formal schema, now familiar, can be used with new, unfamiliar linguistic schemata. Success in the formal educational setting depends on the ability of students to engage in specific communication patterns that require particular types of language organized in certain ways. For struggling L2 learners, both the patterns and their organization are, for the most part, new. Therefore, following the ICF presented in Chapter 2, the teacher needs to build associations between familiar modes of communication and the new ones. Here we focus on one major communication pattern: discussion skills. First, we examine the knowledge and abilities successful participation presupposes. Then we suggest ways to provide scaffolds for this population so that they can participate in this type of classroom discourse.

Academic language refers to both the vocabulary and the language functions of written and spoken discourse typically found in school and official settings. It includes specialized and more formal vocabulary and linguistic functions such as hypothesizing, analyzing, and persuading (Gee, 2007). This academic language differs from the familiar everyday language that most L2 learners first acquire. It is the language of formal schooling, characterized by decontextualized language, with more intricate syntax, academic or subject-specific vocabulary, and complex discourse styles (Cummins, 2001). In addition to such school-based tests, such language is used in testing situations for school transitions to work, professional licenses, or technical certifications. The ways of thinking are expressed in the language through set phrases and words that students need to become familiar with and comfortable using, both orally and in writing.

This language must be explicitly taught in the classroom as a part of encouraging and developing the ways of thinking essential to success in school settings (Scarcella, 2003). Mastering such language is essential for all ELLs (Echevarria, Vogt, & Short, 2008), yet often neglected or seen as beyond the abilities and needs of struggling L2 learners. In classrooms that are based on the ICF, complex language is practiced in a supportive environment with sufficient scaffolding for all students to participate actively. Likewise, academic ways of thinking combined with expressing a range of language functions are an integral part of classroom instruction in the MALP model.

Moving students from general communication to more complex language is no easy task for any L2 learner because it requires wide exposure scaffolded through language instruction and practice (see, e.g., Cummins, 1982; Peregoy & Boyle, 2008 for discussion of basic interpersonal communication skills, BICS). The typical assumption has been that literacy must precede complex language development (Tarone & Bigelow, 2005, 2012). For struggling L2 learners who are more comfortable with and practiced in oral traditions, however, their development of written discourse must be preceded by the acquisition of oral academic discourse. Once these students are able to produce more academic-style oral modes of discourse, they can work on developing the formalistic written modes of classroom language (see Chapter 5).

Mr. Passante designs specific classroom activities so that the students can practice the types of thinking and use the language functions valued in schools. Mr. Passante's goal is to transition the students from their familiar ways of speaking informally to more formal participation in a discussion. Toward this end, Mr. Passante practices discussion skills, a new way of communicating for his class. Although his students have many strengths in the area of oral transmission, they do not feel confident or comfortable participating in a discussion on an academic topic in a classroom setting. He chooses the topic of the Holocaust, which they have previously studied together. To provide scaffolding for this discussion activity, Mr. Passante offers sentence starters for different discourse functions. He gradually introduces these expressions, asking the student to explicitly practice each by incorporating them appropriately into their interactions. Some students need additional sentence frames or complete sentences, which he provides as needed. Without these linguistic scaffolds, students are less able to and less confident about joining in the discussion because they do not have the necessary and appropriate language functions to support their points (Echevarria, Vogt, & Short, 2008; Zwiers, 2007). Similarly, requiring students to use specific language functions provides structure for those students unaccustomed to active participation in discussions. Figure 4.2 shows some functions and accompanying sentence starters.

In addition to scaffolding active participation, Mr. Passante works at intervening only as necessary to give language support, to correct errors that hinder communication, or to add personal observations as appropriate. His goal is to avoid "smoothing over" student discourse or "filling in the gaps" by completing or even pre-empting student utterances, an all too common strategy used by teachers (Musumeci, 1996). While such smoothing over may facilitate clear, comprehensible, fluent discourse, it does not develop students' abilities to engage in discourse and hinders them from practice in producing meaningful utterances in their new language (Walsh, 2002). On the other hand, because Mr. Passante encourages ongoing two-way communication, the students do not hesitate to use him as a resource when questions or problems arise.

Mr. Passante also wants the students to become aware of their participation in the discussion, the expressions they use and the roles that they play, so that they explicitly practice and become comfortable with language functions and partaking in discussions. After each discussion, Mr. Passante asks students to refer to a checklist of language functions he has prepared and posted on the wall to see which of the expressions they used. He also has them consider which

FIGURE 4.2 Sentence Starters

Role in Discussion	Sentence Starter	Sentence Frame	Sentence
Express an opinion	*I think/believe that . . .* *In my opinion . . .*		
Agree with someone	*I agree with you because . . . .*	*I agree with . . . because . . .*	
Disagree with someone	*I don't agree with you because . . .* *I see your point, but . . .*	*I don't agree with . . . because . . .*	
Add to what someone said	*I would like to add that . . .*		
Take a stance	*The reason I feel this would be best is that . . .*		
Ask someone to explain or to clarify			*Could you explain that again?*
Keep talking when someone interrupts			*Please let me finish what I was saying.* *I'd like to complete my thought.*
Finish a thought / discussion			*I'd like to conclude by saying . . .* *I'd like to conclude with . . .*

roles they played in the discussion and which roles they might try in the future. Such reflection is critical in developing students' proficiency in academic ways of thinking and learning (O'Malley & Chamot, 1990; Chamot & O'Malley, 1994) that are often neglected (McCarthy & O'Keeffe, 2004).

When Mr. Passante realizes that a few of the students are not participating regularly, he modifies the activity. Referring back to the ICF and priorities, he realizes that for these students, active participation may not be a priority; they may come from backgrounds that regard the teacher as a central authority who provides the necessary knowledge; they may feel shy, have self-esteem issues, or not feel their language skills are adequate (Brown, 2007; Liang, 2004). However, since in Western-style formal education, active student participation is a priority (Cazden, 1988), Mr. Passante recognizes that he needs to carefully scaffold their involvement and take them to the next level. Here there is no visual support; nevertheless, the general skills they have in oral transmission support them as they follow the flow of the discussion.

Because Mr. Passante has created a climate of mutual trust and respect, the students feel comfortable following his lead in undertaking new activities and in using him as a resource to complete them. In his lesson delivery, he has created interactions in his classroom that are specifically designed to scaffold a new communication pattern building on familiar ones. In his lessons, the new linguistic schemata are the oral discourse functions and expressions, and the new formal schema is group discussion skills. The content remains familiar to the students as they have mastered it previously.

Scaffolding Writing Skills

As the students practice discussion skills and build their ability to articulate the relationships between ideas, the final step is to introduce how these relationships are conveyed in writing. There are many best practices for developing written language for ELLs, many of which are also suitable for struggling L2 learners. The difference is that in MALP classrooms, instruction begins with the oral component and then moves to the written, keeping in mind the MALP guideline of maintaining the explicit connection between oral transmission and the written word.

Often in ESL/EFL classrooms with group work, the teacher or the group appoints one student as a note-taker for the group discussion. More traditionally, students are expected to take notes on their own, and then perhaps write a summary of the discussion. Neither of these approaches is meaningful or appropriate for struggling L2 learners who need to focus on the discussion without the added requirement of processing it and making notations.

Ms. Hertling, in contrast, has her struggling L2 students record the audio for some of their discussions and then asks them to report on their discussion in writing, using their previous recording as the resource. The recording allows them to separate the practice in academic discussion from their analysis and reporting of what was said in their group. This activity also provides an excellent means for Ms. Hertling to help students benefit from her feedback on their writing, as she, too, can refer back to the recording to help them refine their choices with respect to formalistic styles of written discourse as a new genre.

In addition, the teacher can use the reports as a basis for more complex writing and thinking tasks, such as identifying points of consensus versus unresolved issues or finding points in the discussion that could benefit from more elaboration and support. This activity can also lead into a variety of more difficult tasks requiring academic ways of thinking, such as summarizing or synthesizing the discussion.

Underlying the writing instruction, attention must be paid to the sentence level for all L2 learners. Construction of sentences, particularly those with multiple clauses and with transitional words and phrases common to complex written discourse, is particularly challenging for these learners. As noted earlier, they are accustomed to an additive presentation of ideas, one that might lead them to construct sentences without any signals for cohesion and without embedded clauses of any kind. Although many texts exist that teach such writing techniques, they are generally targeted toward advanced learners and/or learners with substantial formal education in their own countries. We suggest a nontraditional approach to the teaching of sentence construction. While the focus of this book is not on sentence-level work, we note here some approaches that show promise for this population.

Spycher (2007), following Martin & Rose (2003) and Schleppegrell (2004), discusses lessons she designed to make explicit linguistic expectations of classroom assignments and the students' language use. For example, Spycher used different graphic organizers to help students with clause and verb analysis. Figure 4.3 shows how a sentence can be analyzed using one of Spycher's organizers.

FIGURE 4.3 Sentence Analysis

Sentence Analysis			
Before the Subject	**Subject**	**Verb**	**After the Verb**
During the 19th century	*Susan B. Anthony*	*was*	*a major figure in the women's rights movement.*
	Her determined struggle	*focused*	*on women's right to own property and to vote.*
	Her efforts	*(finally) led to*	*the 19th Amendment to the U.S. Constitution.*
However,	*Congress*	*did not pass*	*this amendment until 1920, fourteen years after her death.*

Adapted from Spycher (2007, p. 248).

Marshall & DeCapua (2009) describe a method that systematically helps students identify fragments, run-ons, and complete sentences so that they develop an understanding of English written conventions. They call this method Glue because they make the connection to something familiar to students (glue) that joins two items together. Like the glue we use in everyday life, a sentence connector also functions as glue when it joins or connects two independent clauses or an independent and dependent clause. For example, in the following sentence: *The woman is alone, but she doesn't look unhappy because she has a smile on her face*, Marshall and DeCapua would label *but* and *because* as the glue that connects the three clauses in the sentence. The prior sentence would be notated as:

The woman is alone, but she doesn't look unhappy because she has a smile on her face.
S_1 V_1 G S_2 V_2 G S_3 V_3

Step-by-step, Marshall & DeCapua (2009) show how students become familiar with and can apply the basic rule of one glue (connector) for every two independent clauses. This approach will assist them with sentence boundary issues, introduce the types of clause connectors that show relationships other than the additive one, and, in general, give them a means toward reaching some level of sentence variety in their written work.

Test-Taking Skills: Question Formats

Standardized tests, whether mandated K–12 state tests, licensing tests, placement tests or other, presuppose a familiarity with an understanding of academic ways of thinking and formalistic language. Test questions, such as multiple choice or true/false, are examples of decontextualized tasks that produce cultural dissonance for learners who are seeking a meaningful context through which to demonstrate mastery of their knowledge and skills. Figure 4.4 presents how standardized testing reflects the entire Western-style paradigm (see Chapter 3).

For struggling L2 learners to succeed, they will need to demonstrate mastery through standardized assessments, an elusive objective unless they have been able to shift to Western-style formal education and have moved close to the right side of the Ways of Learning Continuum. Although MALP is not designed as a test-preparation approach, there is nonetheless an opportunity to help this

FIGURE 4.4 The Relationship between Western-Style Formal Education and Tests

Central Tenets of Western-Style Formal Education	Tests
Future Relevance	determine future placements, decisions about future education, careers, jobs
Independence	must be administered out of the context of a relationship; often the students' instructor is not—and may not even be permitted to be—the test administrator
Individual Accountability	must be completed individually; no sharing of responsibility at any time during such tests; sharing is seen as cheating
Written Word	with the exception of some oral language proficiency testing, administered in print form, paper or electronically, generally with little or no oral input
Decontextualized Tasks	consist of questions, such as multiple choice, matching; may also include extended response in the form of essays that must follow specific format

population in seeing the rationale behind the tests that they must necessarily take as they progress through a formal educational system. The last part of this chapter examines some of the most widely used testing formats and considers how the scaffolding strategies provided can pave the way for the final step of passing standardized tests.

As should now be evident, for struggling L2 learners, the challenge of "closing the achievement gap" is three-fold. They must develop academic ways of thinking and do so in a language not their own. Furthermore, they must internalize the formats required to demonstrate their mastery of such thinking through testing.

The most common testing formats are generally unknown to these learners; even those highly educated in their home countries may not be familiar with these techniques. We refer to closed-ended test questions—that is, questions that limit responses from which test takers choose the one correct answer. Inherent in such questions are linguistic and cultural issues (Menken, 2008), including the fact that test takers must be able to interpret the question according to the perspective of the creator of the test questions.

These closed-ended questions contrast with open-ended test questions that require longer responses in which the test-taker supplies necessary information and where more than one way of formulating one's answer is possible. Test takers are expected to explain their knowledge, give examples, and demonstrate mastery in their responses.

Here we investigate two types of common closed-ended test formats— true/false questions and multiple choice questions—and consider the assumptions underlying such questions. It is important to emphasize that we believe it is not simply a question of teaching the learner how to answer such items. We argue instead that learning to do well on these types of test formats is part of the fundamental shift from the left side of the Ways of Learning Continuum to the right side. Learning how to answer such questions, although somewhat challenging, is not so difficult; what *is* difficult is for students to grasp that they cannot rely on their ideas, their opinions, and their experiences in the world when responding to these questions and that they must refer to specific material that has been taught in class. Careful scaffolding of ideas will help with any standardized test-taking, whether in school, for work, for citizenship, or any other.

When confronting assessments, students from oral cultures look for familiar signs and see instead only unfamiliar and disconnected text with questions that seem to have no basis in the real world they know. In training Haitian future home health aides and certified nurse's aides, it has been our experience through test-preparation and item analysis after the exams that these learners often used their own personal experiences to determine answers to questions rather than what they had seen in a textbook or learned about in class. They believed that what they knew for a fact trumped what they had been only told about or read. This belief occurred even when they did recall what they had been taught. However, they had not been coached to avoid their own real-world experience and to focus only on the material in the course when responding. This coaching is counter to their learning paradigm and yet, without it, they fail the exam. As evident from this example, struggling L2 learners intuitively connect with prior knowledge. Again the priorities clash: from their perspective, real-world experience is paramount, in direct contrast to our focus on determining understanding and measuring achievement through decontextualized standardized testing. The cultural dissonance often leads to the "achievement gap."

Scaffolding Multiple Choice Questions

Developed in the early 20th century, multiple choice questions have become the most widely used standardized testing format in Western-style formal education (Lemann, 2000). The questions ask students to select the correct answer from a given choice, usually a list of three or four, where only one is correct and the others, which are distractors, are wrong answers.

To introduce struggling L2 learners to this type of assessment, the teacher begins with something familiar. In Mrs. Ortega's class, the students had previously presented collages about themselves. These collages are hanging on the walls around the classroom. Mrs. Ortega takes some of the items from their collages and writes them on the board. As she writes the name of each item, she points to it on one of the collages to reinforce meaning and print. Next, she writes the following sentence and lists four items, only one of which is found on Omar's collage:

Omar likes:

ice cream

dancing

rap music

Hello Kitty

Mrs. Ortega then asks the students to choose the correct answer from the list. The students know the correct answer is *rap music* because they see it was the only one of the four items in his collage. After the teacher has practiced this with other students' names and other items from the collages, she adds *a, b, c,* and *d* before the choices and asks the students to respond using only the letter. Once they are comfortable with this, the next step is to provide new material and ask the same question. The answer is in the material rather than from their personal experience.

Jean has to go to the store. Should he walk, take a bus, take a train, or ride in his friend's car? He decides to walk.

How does Jean get to the store?
   a. bus
   b. train
   c. walk
   d. ride in a car

This activity demonstrates how in school we ask about new information obtained from oral/written sources and not from personal experience. Once the task itself is familiar to them, they are ready to handle new material in this format.

In classroom settings today, however, there is an expectation that all students will be able to perform academic tasks using academic language in their L2 to demonstrate academic ways of thinking (Cottrell, 2001; National Research Council, 2007).

Applying a concept means using it to demonstrate mastery of new content through that concept. Here we focus on building understanding of the concepts underlying the common tasks demanded in the classroom. Referring to Bloom's Taxonomy (1956) facilitates our work because we can take each of the types of thinking and show how to develop it so students can access the language and content in the lessons they are exposed to in school.

Scaffolding True/False Questions

True or false is a common task in many classrooms. Such questions are often used to see if students can identify which statements of fact are correct. For struggling L2 learners from the left side of the Ways of Learning Continuum, such questions have little or no meaning. Their perspective is "teach me what I need to learn and I will learn it," and "don't teach me what isn't true."

To scaffold true/false questions so that learners understand how to answer them, the class can begin (Mrowicki, 1990) with simple yes/no questions about the students in the class: Does Carmen have a sister? Does Vuong have a brother? Does Yasmin have a cell phone? The students answer, using yes or no. All three schemata are familiar in this initial step.

Next, the teacher rephrases the questions as statements and asks the students to supply yes or no, either orally or in writing.

Carmen has a sister.	Yes____	No ____
Vuong has a brother.	Yes____	No ____
Yasmin has a cell phone.	Yes____	No ____

Once this activity has been completed, the teacher introduces the terms *true* for yes and *false* for no, explaining that these words are the ones commonly used in school:

Carmen has a sister.	True____ False ____
Vuong has a brother.	True____ False ____
Yasmin has a cell phone.	True____ False ____

Finally, the teacher introduces new content that the students may or may not know:

Beijing is the capital of China.	True ____ False ____
Istanbul is the capital of Turkey.	True ____ False ____
Melbourne is the capital of Australia.	True ____ False ____

At this point, students are familiar with the task and the teacher can confidently say that the response is an indication relating to content mastery and not to the academic language or the type of task being used to elicit a response.

Once the students can readily respond to literal true/false questions, the teacher will need to develop questions that incorporate higher-level thinking skills into the true/false format. For example, if the students have been learning about the capitals of different countries, the teacher could practice:

The capital of Turkey has a larger population than the capital of China.	True ____ False ____
The capital of Australia has a smaller population than the capital of Turkey.	True ____ False ____
The capital of China has a larger population than the capital of Australia.	True ____ False ____

This overview of two popular test-taking formats and scaffolding them under MALP is not teaching test preparation *per se* but rather is another step in developing struggling L2 learners' understanding of the kinds of thinking and types of tasks used in schools. A natural outgrowth will be that they will be able to participate in classroom activities, and, subsequently, classroom and other assessments.

Teaching students to understand and respond as expected in Western-style formal educational settings requires an appreciation of the differing priorities inherent in their learning paradigm. As we saw with Mr. Mancuso and Diego at the beginning of this chapter, it was the clash of priorities that prevented them from effectively communicating. Given the program demands teachers face, they may find it difficult to focus first on scaffolding new ways of thinking and academic language. However, it is a focus on new ways of thinking and responding that will facilitate content mastery as the content is embedded in decontextualized tasks. Knowing this will help teachers to take a step back before expecting students to respond to the common, "define X" task and will ensure that they implement the careful scaffolding described in this chapter.

5

Designing Projects

Mrs. Janssen found that her students were unfamiliar with talking about dates and the calendar, so she decided to design a project to help them become comfortable with these concepts. She chose to base the project on their birthdays, a template that she had heard about previously (DeCapua & Marshall, 2011). Although the idea for this project came from the discussion of the timeline project by DeCapua & Marshall (2011), Mrs. Janssen adapted it to meet the needs of her learners.

> Mrs. Janssen began with January and wrote the months on the board, asking if anyone had a birthday in January. Silvia nodded. Mrs. Janssen then asked Silvia what day in January and Silvia held up 10 fingers. Then the other students called out "ten." Mrs. Janssen then said and wrote on the board next to January—*Silvia's birthday is January 10*. Then Silvia began, "one, nine . . . " Another student said 19. Then the class together spoke briefly about finding out the year in which they were born, which had not been Mrs. Janssen's plan, but was something the students decided to add. This became a project about math as well because they had to figure out ages and years, and many of them had not done this before. As they continued, and came to March, no one the class had a birthday in that month, but Anita raised her hand and said, "my daughter." Another student asked, "How old your daughter?" She answered, "eight." The class then put together a sentence about Anita's daughter, which Mrs. Janssen wrote on the board. By the end of the activity, for each month there were several sentences with birthdays of students or members of their families. Even a visitor to the class was included in this project. The class repeated each sentence as Mrs. Janssen pointed to the words. Some

students copied only their own birthday sentence into their note-books; other, more advanced students copied several, or, in some cases, all the birthdays. The class worked on this project during two class sessions with Mrs. Janssen taking photos of the board to preserve their work.

What teachers take for granted as the norm can present significant challenges for students with different priorities and a different knowledge base. In many cultures, birthdays are not considered important or interesting (Gahungo, Gahungo, & Luseno, 2011). However, a lesson on birthdays can provide both cultural background about how and when birthdays become significant and new knowledge about time, numbers, and the calendar (DeCapua & Marshall, 2011). For example, birthdays help students to learn the distinction between ordinal and cardinal numbers. In addition, students need to attend to the format for writing dates. In the United States, the norm is month, day, and year (April 26, 2012), while the British write day, month, and year (26 April, 2012), and Koreans write year, month, and date (2012, April, 26). Birthdays in the developed world are important for myriad government, school, and work-related forms, all of which struggling L2 learners need to complete at some point in their lives.

What Is Project-Based Learning?

The series of activities that Mrs. Janssen was conducting constituted what we refer to as a MALP project. Project-based learning views instruction as the development of knowledge and skills in service of a culminating student product that demonstrates mastery. It integrates different language skills and knowledge, promoting the acquisition of both linguistic and content information. Learners do not immediately master the vocabulary, structures, and information they are taught, but need multiple opportunities to practice these consistently in different contexts in order to truly master them (Gass & Selinker, 2008). A project on birthdays is ideal for illustrating how lesson ideas can be used in different contexts.

Project-based learning is ideal for integrating MALP into classes for struggling L2 learners. As described by DeCapua & Marshall (2011, p. 84), it:

- encourages immediate relevance and interconnectedness
- allows for differentiation
- supports group work while requiring individual accountability

- easily integrates oral transmission and print
- provides a framework for introducing, practicing, and recycling language, content, and ways of thinking.

Project-based learning also aligns with the work of Vygotsky (1978). He argues that learning occurs when there is interaction with carefully scaffolded learning activities that challenge students without being too difficult to discourage them. In addition, in project-based learning, peer interaction is central, and establishing interpersonal communication skills is important since learners often learn best from their peers (Blum-Kulka, Huck-Taglicht, & Avni, 2004).

Project-based learning consists of these steps:

- selecting a project
- identifying the tasks, skills, and materials needed
- evaluating those student skills relevant to the project and delegating project tasks
- implementing the project
- sharing the finished project.

Because project-based learning is intended to be recursive and ongoing, a final step is to reflect on and evaluate the project in order to propose and plan subsequent projects (see DeCapua & Marshall, 2011, for a detailed account of project-based learning and MALP).

When we refer to a MALP project, we have specific types of projects in mind. In order to transition learners to Western-style formal education and to help them adjust to an individualistic cultural orientation, MALP projects must incorporate all three components and the six elements of MALP. To ensure that she is doing this, Mrs. Janssen refers to the MALP chart and Checklist, with the conditions, processes, and activities for learning. We can analyze her project by referring to each component of the model, along with its elements.

Immediate Relevance and Interconnectedness

Since the students are describing birthdays, they are talking with their classmates about themselves and their family members. As they share personal information with each other and with Mrs. Janssen, their relationships grow and strengthen, making learning immediately relevant, and fostering interconnectedness. By accepting these conditions for learning for her students, Mrs. Janssen is paving the way for successful learning.

Shared and Individual Responsibility

Students participated by providing their own and family members' birthdays. The class as a whole worked together on reading and recording the information.

Oral Transmission with Print

Mrs. Janssen wrote as the students shared their dates. Then the class read from the board. Finally, they wrote their own data into their notebooks and some of the stronger students also included their classmates' birthdays. By incorporating individual responsibility and group responsibility in the project, and by using oral transmission to promote reading and writing, Mrs. Janssen combined their preferred processes with those of the classroom.

Academic Ways of Thinking with Familiar Language and Context

Mrs. Janssen scaffolded the new concepts—calendar, dates, and format—and content, birthdays. All three components and six elements of MALP were in place as part of Mrs. Janssen's instructional plans, which she developed with frequent reference to the MALP Checklist.

Making Literacy a Meaningful Process

MALP projects may focus on the development of specific skills. The basic skills of learning to read are a necessary part of the curriculum for struggling L2 learners. Designing a MALP project focused on literacy necessarily begins with a reexamination of literacy, not only as a skill but as a process for learning. Struggling L2 learners need to find a meaningful way to approach their new language through print because they are new to literacy.

In addition to teaching literacy skills, teachers need to help students learn to invest literacy with new purposes: reading and writing have practical, utilitarian uses and also aesthetic purposes. By engaging in reading for both learning and for enjoyment, students acquire the language of schooling (Krashen, 2004). MALP projects encourage students to experience reading and writing together in a meaningful way that taps into academic tasks and the language associated with those tasks.

As we saw in Mrs. Janssen's class, beginning-level L2 learners were able to recognize and produce the sentence pattern _____'s *birthday is* _____ _____, _____, as in *Silvia's birthday is January 10, 1981.* It was meaningful practice because it contained information about an actual student or family member of one of the students. The students felt connected to print and began to take ownership of this sentence pattern.

By creating MALP projects that infuse reading and writing skills, the teacher can strengthen the connection between the students and literacy. Students begin to see themselves as readers and writers and embrace these new roles in the context of the classroom. MALP projects can be conducted recursively, allowing students to revisit the same types of tasks to develop competence and generate increasingly more accomplished products. In a subsequent class, Mrs. Janssen asked the students to create a page of the birthdays of the people in their families. She asked them to use the familiar sentence pattern and added an additional pattern to create another level of difficulty and expand the project, _____ is _____. Mrs. Jansseen modeled by writing the sentence frames using her information: *My birthday is June 20, 1978. I am 35. My son's birthday is March 19, 2003. He is 10.*

Equally essential is that teachers convey to this population the concept of text as communication between the author and an audience. Initially, the learners find it difficult to think of text as having been created by a person who had a purpose for reaching out to an audience concerning a topic. In looking at this process, teachers assist such learners to make connections to print by teaching them how to discern the author's topic, purpose, and audience. By creating their own text as a class, they begin conceptualizing text in these terms using their own topic, discussing their purpose, and identifying an audience for their work. Then they can move into extracting meaning from the text of others.

There are many examples of literacy projects in ESL classes—such as autobiographies, personal essays on experiences coming to this country, or descriptions of family members—that draw on material already known to the students, making the content familiar and lessening the cognitive load. One useful way to structure writing activities for this population is to use the Language Experience Approach, or LEA, originally developed for teaching reading to native speakers of English (Van Allen & Allen, 1967). This approach has, since its inception, undergone various adaptations for use with ELLs, and has been quite successful with these students (DeCapua, Smathers, & Tang, 2009; Dixon & Nessel, 1990).

The LEA, when implemented as a MALP project, allows for the balancing of the three schemata—linguistic, content, and formal—and helps to demystify literacy skills. It is an instance where identified best practices can be viewed and fully understood through the lens of the MALP model of instruction. The LEA takes an experience the class has participated in together as the point of departure for developing literacy. The language and content are familiar because the students are using language to recall and retell what they already know about, heard about, or have experienced. In Chapter 3, we saw how Mr. Morris and his students shared orally and in writing family information through personal photos. That activity was an example of using LEA as part of a MALP lesson. The teacher guided the class through the LEA, promoting interconnectedness in his class and providing an effective way to transition students from the oral mode to the written word.

Before Ms. Acevedo was trained in MALP, she taught her adult class very traditionally. She focused on such tasks as having students take turns reading sentences aloud, correcting their pronunciation, and explaining vocabulary words while the students copied the definitions. After she was MALP-trained, her class became a different place. In this example, Ms. Acevedo has taken a common ESL lesson idea, cooking and recipes, and created a literacy project.

Day 1

My students loved to talk about food. I thought that this would be a great way to segue into a MALP project. My students (and the rest of the school) knew that something different was happening that day when I greeted them in a hat and apron and had all sorts of cooking realia on the desk.

We started out by going over cooking terms, written crossword answer style. To help them understand these, I used the realia, such as a blender and a whisk, that I had brought in. Many of these items had come up in our previous discussions about food and cooking. Before the class, I had also noted on the board the pages in the picture dictionary for food terms, which a couple of my students used as a reference to find the English word for what they wanted to refer to.

Day 2

At our next class, I brought in some common recipes from different countries. As we discussed these recipes, we had flash cards and index cards with most of the ingredients on them for the students to refer to.

Day 3

This time, I demonstrated my Mom's potato salad recipe, using realia and flash cards. Then we had students demonstrating their recipes. We also went over the instructions for other recipes of mine and those of students who were absent that day. It was important to check that all the recipes flowed logically and that they included all the information needed for someone else to prepare the dish. When they shared their recipes with someone who was unfamiliar with the dish, they were often surprised at how much they assumed others would know. It opened their eyes to the need to be explicit for even the smallest detail. Once we finished, I typed everyone's recipe and shared everyone's recipes.

Implementing the Writing Process with MALP

As discussed in the ICF, a priority of formal education is that students come to value literacy as a process for communicating. In MALP projects, literacy is seen not as merely a set of skills. This view is a major shift for struggling L2 learners who typically view writing as copying and not as a creative activity that they can themselves engage in. The purpose of text, both accessing it and developing it, must become meaningful for them.

As part of creating long-term projects that go beyond the sentence level in complexity, students engage in the writing process. It is useful to examine the nature of this process viewed from the learner's perspective, as it represents an unfamiliar, or at least less preferred formal schema for them. For all students, but particularly for those who are new to the printed word or not comfortable in extracting meaning from print, breaking writing into stages is consistent with MALP and facilitates their ease with this new schema. The writing process commonly consists of five stages: pre-writing, drafting, revising, editing, and publishing (Calkins, 1994; Ferris & Hedgcock, 2004).

The first stage, pre-writing, includes several oral elements. In this stage, students select a topic, brainstorm ideas for their topic, and then, with the teacher's assistance, organize these ideas into some logical structure. In the second stage, drafting, the students create the text. This stage can also be accomplished orally, with the teacher transcribing their words. The third and fourth stages, revising and editing, require the students to review the written version of their work so as to improve it; the distinction between these stages lies in the scope and focus of the changes being considered. In the final stage, publishing, the students share their work with others. Through the writing process students learn how to develop from start to finish a polished document and they become authors.

Another way to increase student engagement with MALP projects is to take advantage of options now available through the use of technology in instruction. Increasingly, we find the tools of technology being used in classrooms. For example, teachers and struggling L2 learners can take advantage of digitalized storytelling, in which narrative is combined with digital content. This content can be as simple as using still images and text on slides or video and music. Digitalized storytelling is essentially the application of technology to traditional modes of sharing narratives and has been recognized to be a powerful motivator in and tool for language and knowledge building (Vinogradova, Linville, & Bickel, 2011).

To create digital stories, learners must be familiar with basic computer skills. If they are not comfortable using a computer, language learning activities can be combined with simple technical lessons.

When Ms. Acevedo's students had completed writing their demonstration projects and had mastered computer basics, they began developing their digital stories, choosing to use PowerPoint. Working in pairs, the students entered text into the slides and searched for and added appropriate images. Later in the term, after the students had become more competent in digital storytelling, they recorded the story, taking turns reading different slides. A class narratives project like this one can provide the foundation for other projects, such as theme booklets introduced later in this chapter.

Creating Curriculum through Student Needs and Interests

Through learner-generated material, struggling L2 learners will master classroom skills and become comfortable with decontextualized tasks in order to transfer that learning to more unfamiliar material. In a MALP classroom, when literacy is introduced through project-based learning, students will themselves design meaningful literacy activities that serve their needs while helping them develop academic ways of thinking. We have seen this with Mrs. Janssen and Ms. Acevedo in this chapter.

Auerbach (1989) suggests that projects begin with a stage in which the teacher listens to students to hear what their concerns are and structures activities in class to elicit student comments and issues; then student themes are explored and used to extend language and literacy issues by connecting the content to relevant language. Learners who often find consistent attendance difficult become more engaged in the process of learning in their new classroom setting when they are active, rather than passive, recipients of the instruction (Marshall, DeCapua, & Antolini, 2010). The teachers examined here were able to shift the responsibility to the students. It was the students who provided the real information about people, places, and events familiar to them. The teacher-student interactions were an authentic exchange of information and naturally engaged the students in speaking, reading, and writing. A personal investment in learning develops an important sense of ownership among learners, as theme booklet projects demonstrate.

Theme Booklets

In our discussion of how to design MALP projects, we have focused on projects of limited scope, such as creating posters or telling a story. A common concern is how to implement extended literacy projects with struggling L2 learners with very limited literacy skills. When carefully scaffolded, a class project based on the creation of a booklet around some theme of common interest encourages and supports literacy development. We refer to these extended literacy projects as theme booklets. Theme booklets are organized collections of information that students gather and prepare in written form on a specific topic. When students have very limited literacy skills and/or language proficiency, theme booklets primarily consist of photos, each introduced by a heading and accompanied by a few sentences. Theme booklets can be incorporated in a variety of ways that support and interface with the curriculum and when carefully implemented with the Checklist as a guide are in keeping with MALP. Another benefit of theme booklets is that the students are creating a library of their own work. The booklets can be placed in a bookcase (rolling cart/carrier) and organized, which adds to stronger categorization skills.

Theme booklets are an excellent tool for helping struggling L2 learners with limited or no literacy understand and become familiar with the design and layout of non-fiction books. Mrs. Manetta used booklets to introduce her students to the different parts and overall organization of books, including table of contents, chapter or section headings, and an index. Mrs. Manetta chose a short, non-fiction book, and she photocopied the title page, table of contents, two representative chapters, and the index. She taped the different pages together to form a long scroll and the taped it to the wall. The class examined the different parts, along with the actual book. Students were encouraged to walk along the "scroll" and point to the different parts with the names. The "scroll" allowed the students to see the different parts of a book all at once and visually understand how a non-fiction book is structured (www.textmapping.org).

We categorize MALP theme booklets into three types: (1) curriculum-based booklets that focus on content schemata; (2) procedural booklets that focus on formal schemata, explaining processes such as school routines; (3) language booklets that focus on linguistic schemata, developing writing skills to support academic ways of thinking.

The instructor's focus in guiding the students as they develop theme booklets is twofold. First, this is an opportunity for the students to collaborate on a MALP project that develops their literacy. Second, it provides scaffolding for the development of new schemata appropriate to the type of booklet they are making.

The next section examines sample theme booklets designed for each of the three schemata. In each case, the instructor was guided by the MALP chart and Checklist. As we examine these booklets, which focus on building subject matter schemata, we detail the process for producing any type of theme booklet.

Curriculum-Based Booklets

Themes are drawn from topics students are encountering in their learning. For example, Ms. Anton focused on biographies of famous people as a tie-in to her social studies unit. In her history class, the students needed to know about famous historical figures (DeCapua & Marshall, 2011; Marshall, DeCapua, & Antolini, 2010). The students began by choosing and learning about a famous person from their own country, such as a respected political or religious leader, a freedom fighter, or a women's rights activist. Once they had mastered how to prepare and write a short biography, Ms. Anton had them prepare biographies about important historical figures in their new country. Their work led to the creation of a Famous People theme booklet. Similarly, learners preparing for the citizenship test can create theme booklets on important historical, geographical, and political facts.

Basing theme booklets on the curriculum gives students the opportunity to process what they are learning, create a document that can serve as a review of the material, and offer help to students as they master new content being covered in the curriculum. It also gives the teacher valuable information about students' abilities to prioritize the new concepts, transfer learning to new situations, as well as clear up any misconceptions about the material that become evident as the students plan, create, and design their booklet. To help understand the process, let us take a look at Mrs. Tian's adult basic education class and how she worked with her students to create a curriculum-based theme booklet.

It is Fire Prevention Week. Last year, Mrs. Tian used the chapter in her pre-scribed text, which included:

- a short description of a hypothetical fire situation
- emergency phone numbers
- basic vocabulary related to fire and rooms of the house
- line drawings of the family, the apartment, and the fire scene
- true/false questions and fill-in-the-blank with a word bank, which is similar to a matching activity.

From past experience, Mrs. Tian knew that the students found the chapter uninteresting, even though she supplemented it with print materials she located in the community and online. After her MALP training, she wanted to find a way to make the fire prevention information engaging and relevant (without starting a fire!) She wondered what could be done instead of using the tradi-tional book exercises to allow students to rely on their personal experience and what they had learned from each other and the teacher.

Step One: Planning

The theme booklet needs to be planned and tasks assigned. An important part of this step is for the students to decide how to delegate responsibility. The four phases each include several different tasks, which can be distributed according to abilities, skills, and interests. Teachers must ensure that some of the tasks involve shared responsibility while others involve individual accountability and that oral transmission is combined with print from the outset. For example, when the students brainstorm topics, teachers list them and students read them back.

> Mrs. Tian began by describing the day her cousin's kitchen had an oil fire. She didn't have a fire extinguisher but she had baking soda, which she threw on the burning oil. As she recounted the story, she held up a kitchen fire extinguisher and a box of baking soda. Then she passed around the two items for the students to look at, touch, and taste.

The students then exchanged personal experiences of other dangerous situa-tions that caused fires: Nadeen told the class how her cousin had a fire when she forgot the iron was on because her baby cried; Sonia described how having too many appliances plugged into an extension cord triggered a small fire in her mother's house; Marcos talked about how careless smoking started grass fires. These experiences formed the basis for creating their curriculum theme booklet, Fire Prevention and Reporting.

The class prepared a wall calendar to help them plan the schedule for the project to reinforce the concepts of time, planning, and scheduling. Posting the schedule on the class calendar where everyone can see it, refer to it, and check off completed tasks, is a good way to keep everyone focused and on track.

Step Two: Creating

This phase is in many ways the heart of the project and the one in which most of the new academic thinking and literacy skills will be developed. Students search for sources of information, select what they need, and generate text for their booklets.

An effective starting point, particularly for students with very limited literacy, is the selection of visuals that will be complemented by text. This differs from the more traditional approach to such a project where the starting point tends to be the text with visuals then selected to accompany that text. Visuals can include maps, diagrams, drawings, and tables.

After the students gather visuals and/or the data for their booklet, they write the appropriate accompanying text. Although writing is daunting for struggling L2 learners, text is fundamental to theme booklets. Teachers must provide scaffolding that will allow these students to be successful as writers. Initially, teachers can use LEA strategies, beginning with oral input and creating group writing. They can also provide sentence frames that align with the visuals the students have chosen. During the creating phase, teachers conduct lessons that introduce and build on the stages of the writing process. The collection of information becomes part of the pre-writing stage. They may make a list of questions, a list of items to include, or they may make a cluster map of ideas that relate. These activities are executed collectively, in pairs, in small groups, or with the class as a whole. Teachers write the student contributions on the board, which they copy to use as reference for their individual drafts. In this way, the students have completed the pre-writing stage, which includes selecting a topic, brainstorming and gathering information, and organizing it in some logical way.

After pre-writing, students create a draft, whether simple sentences, short paragraphs, or longer text. Teachers emphasize that at this stage it is more important that they write something than that they be concerned about producing a perfect product.

When the students have completed their initial drafts, either individually or together with others, they are ready to work on revising for meaning. An important strategy for all writers as they revise and edit is to read their work out loud. For those who come from oral backgrounds, this step is especially essential. The reader does not need to be the student who wrote the text, but can be the teacher or another student. For the read-aloud, teachers can provide hard copies or project the text electronically so that students can follow along with the reader.

In Step Two, students also focus on logical sequencing. Even if they are only preparing two or three simple sentences, they need to put these in some order. In addition to reviewing the content and logic of their writing, students must also check for accuracy. This sharing of ideas when fact-checking and researching prepares them to later work on academic tasks on their own. Let's return to Mrs. Tian's class.

Each student in Mrs. Tian's class chose a situation and either drew it or found a picture in a magazine or online to illustrate that particular fire hazard. Mrs. Tian supplied the term *fire hazard*, which they put at the top of each page. Subsequently, Mrs. Tian asked the class about their experiences with emergencies, and one student called out the local emergency number to call for help. Together they shared the information needed orally as Mrs. Tian wrote it on the board: the address, the room in the house affected, and their name:

I am calling about a fire at _____.

It is in the _____.

My name is _____.

The students used this information to continue preparing their Fire Prevention and Reporting theme booklet. The students copied the sentence frames onto the pages they had prepared with their pictures and added their personal information in the blank spaces. This fill-in-the-blank activity, where they would enter their own information, was meaningful to them, unlike the fictitious example in the class textbook. Later the class used their pages to practice asking and answering each other, using the information they entered.

Where are you located/what is your address?

Where is the fire located?

Do you have a fire extinguisher?

What is your name?

Who else is in the house with you?

Step Three: Designing and Disseminating

In this third phase, the students plan the form and appearance of the theme booklet. They may want to draw a special cover or include a particular photo. If they have different sections in their booklet, students may want to include a table of contents. The Fire Prevention and Reporting Booklet, from Mrs. Tian's class had two sections: How to Prevent a Fire and How to Report a Fire. The cover had photo of a fire engine, a fire fighter, and the emergency call number.

Once the design has been completed, the theme booklet can be shared with people outside of the class. The class can make a bulletin board display, distribute hard copies to members of the school community and their families, and/or disseminate electronic copies via a class website, blog, or other online location. By having a real audience reading their product, struggling L2 students become vested as writers and print becomes a meaningful form of communication (Marshall & DeCapua, 2009).

As they create theme booklets, struggling L2 learners share personal experiences, building relationships as they learn about each other. They develop the language that describes the situation and practice critical-thinking skills using the typical classroom exercises that they have been learning using familiar language and content from other lessons. In addition, the booklet provides a model and a reference for other students entering the program.

Procedural Booklets

These theme booklets target a process or set of procedures that students need to know or that they have studied but need to review. A popular topic for theme booklets is about the school they are attending. This booklet can be for their own use, as well as a resource for new students. They may decide to prepare a booklet describing basic classroom procedures, such as how to sharpen a pencil, one explaining the roles of different school support personnel and offices, such as the attendance office, or one depicting community resources, such as the local library (Marshall & DeCapua, 2009).

Many students in Mr. Safa's class wanted to learn about the logistics of getting a driver's permit and driver's license. Because of financial and other constraints, they were unable to visit the Department of Motor Vehicles, so Mr. Safa showed a *YouTube* clip demonstrating the process.

Because Mr. Safa's students wanted to get their driver's permits and driver's licenses, they practiced using such phrases as

I need _____

I have to _____

As they moved into revision, the students focused on, as described earlier, relevance, order, details, and accuracy. In a draft of the Driver's License theme booklet, several of the students had added sentences about experiences family members or friends had had with the Department of Motor Vehicles. Often struggling L2 learners try to present everything they experienced, rather than providing only necessary, important, and/or relevant information (De Capua & Marshall, 2010a). While this is true of many inexperienced writers, and even some native speakers (Collins, 1998), for struggling L2 learners much of it is related to their unfamiliarity with academic ways of thinking and English story structure. Guided by Mr. Safa, the students identified the sentences that were not directly related to the topic of how to get a driver's permit and driver's license and eliminated them.

In cases where sentences are not in a logical order or are irrelevant, yet the students do not seem to realize this, teachers will need to work with them on organization and relevance. Linear organization in writing, similar to our Western linear conceptualization of time, is not universal, and some students will know different rhetorical styles (Hofling, 1993; Noor, 2001). Using the MALP Checklist to guide his lesson planning, Mr. Safa helped the class recognize the steps in applying for a driver's permit and driver's license. He ensured that they had included all essential steps, described them in detail, and sequenced them logically. Whether teacher-prompted or student-generated, this process of ordering story information introduces and/or reinforces the academic tasks of sequencing and logical order and identifying relevant and irrelevant information.

In Mrs. Stein's class, students prepared a welcome theme booklet (Marshall & DeCapua, 2009) for new arrivals, with photos, captions, and general information about the kinds of things they wished someone had told them when they first arrived. This booklet, unlike most material for newcomers, was prepared by students who could relate to the problems and needs of the newest arrivals to the area. Often orientation materials are overly detailed, not available in students' native language, or found scattered in many different offices and agencies. A student-produced theme booklet is an invaluable resource for new students.

Mrs. Stein chose to focus on school routines. Recently arrived students may need help in basic school routines, ranging from using lockers and combination locks or attendance sheets, to how to log on to the school computers (DeCapua, Smaehers, & Tang, 2009). In many secondary schools, when students arrive after the official start of the school day, they are required to go to the main office and sign in via an attendance sheet. Since this is something many newly arrived struggling L2 learners are unfamiliar with, Ms. Stein's students included a page with a photo of the office, a photo of the attendance sheet, and a sentence explaining what to do.

The preparation of this type of booklet involves collecting data in English, writing it, wrestling with the problem of what is relevant for new arrivals, and how to best present it in the theme booklet. Providing newcomers with a useful tool makes these students producers of written materials for consumption within their community. Furthermore, since such a welcome booklet will need to be updated periodically, this is a project that different classes in different years can build on as they update the information.

Language Booklets

This type of booklet focuses on structures and vocabulary of the new language to help students process and master them. Its purpose is to develop the language that is used in school and parallels the ways of thinking expected in school settings. Struggling L2 learners find moving to this type of language quite challenging as the concepts underlying the language are themselves new. By producing theme booklets that highlight this increasingly complex language, the students gain confidence in using it. As for all MALP projects, the schemata are balanced so that the content and organization of the booklet will be familiar while the language will be the unfamiliar schema that the teacher is guiding the class through.

In Mrs. Jones' class, students were talking about the teachers in the school, so she brought up the website for the school and clicked on Mr. Paul's photo. The students reacted with comments about Mr. Paul, whom many of them already knew. She asked them to say what they knew about him and listed the information on the board. She then saw an opportunity to use descriptions working on comparison and contrast; she asked them to suggest the name of another teacher and found that photo on the website also. Next she brainstormed descriptions with them for the second teacher, Ms. Sanyal. She asked them to name one item that was on both description lists, as well as one item on each that was not present on the other list. This set up the similarities and differences, a concept that Ms. Sanyal had already worked on with the class earlier in the year.

Mrs. Jones introduced common comparison-contrast sentence patterns. Guided by sentence frames provided by Mrs. Jones, the students created sentences about the two teachers in preparation for a theme booklet incorporating the language of comparison and contrast.

Producing a theme booklet of this type is a MALP alternative to the more traditional approach of using textbook exercises and worksheets to teach language. Each student selected a familiar topic and worked on a page for the booklet. José, for instance, was interested in cars and decided to compare and contrast two models he especially liked, while Suzanna decided to look at two fast food chains popular among the students.

Integrating MALP into the Curriculum

Learning standards and mandated or scripted curricula with scope and sequence have become the norm with teachers and are required to adhere to instructional mandates. Because MALP is an instructional model designed to provide a framework for instruction, it is not tied to specific standards. Meeting these standards and benchmarks in no way conflicts with MALP, which can be used with any content and, therefore, any curriculum. Teachers will be able to integrate MALP into their teaching, regardless of the requirements of their program of studies. For example, for K–12 grades in the United States, there are federal Common Core Standards for the subject areas at the different grade levels, as well as individual state standards. Similarly, for adult education, standards and assessments are mandated by the National Reporting System (NRS). Canadian Benchmarks have slightly more flexible approaches to standards and assessments, but also have some across-the-board expectations in terms of the material to be mastered at various grades and language and literacy proficiency levels.

Given these realities, how can teachers follow a MALP model implementing MALP projects and create a MALP classroom? For adolescents and adults, effective programs are those that have immediate relevance to their own lives, relying on authentic materials whenever possible (Kağitçibaşi, Göksen, & Gülgöz, 2005; Lynch, 2009). It is essential to create authentic, relevant materials to complement required ones so that struggling L2 learners can connect in a real-world sense to the course content.

In designing a MALP project for secondary school students, the teacher must begin with the mandated state standards. We observed this in the discussion of Ms. Anton's biography theme booklet based on the social studies curriculum. The standards may be specific for ELLs or may be general standards for a content area or some combination. Using the standards aligns with MALP because they identify the knowledge and skills required of students. The skills will parallel the academic ways of thinking essential for MALP implementation, but the knowledge will be a challenge. It is important that the teacher find links to the learner's background for the specific areas of knowledge the curriculum requires. If the curriculum asks for the learner to master language and content that is initially inaccessible, the teacher can construct, through MALP projects, ways to transition the learner into that language and content. In Ms. Giorno's high school social studies class, for example, the textbook included readings on cultural diffusion that her students were largely unable to access. Adapting text works sometimes, but it typically results in readable but still meaningless material for learners who are not yet used to or comfortable with extracting meaning from print. With MALP, the teacher can keep the headings of the text, the illustrations, and charts or tables, and construct an activity to develop understanding of cultural diffusion, a universal process. Ms. Giorno used the example of music and asked the students how they saw different types of music spreading in their own lives and communities. They were able to use the headings as a guide to their discussion and later, for their reports.

Many adult education programs also have selected specific programs, textbooks, and materials that are mandated for use in their classes. When teachers are given such mandates, it is difficult for them to make lessons meaningful. Integrating MALP is an excellent way to make the mandated materials come alive. As Wrigley and Powrie (2002) point out, the keys to success with adult literacy students include their making an investment in the program and taking ownership of the content as meaningful to them.

By including MALP projects along with the textbook in the curriculum, teachers are able to maximize the many benefits of MALP and at the same time cover the mandated points from the curriculum. Mr. Thomas, for instance, was required to use a popular ESL textbook. Before he was MALP-trained, he focused on working through the chapter on family from the textbook where the students had to ask and answer questions about an imaginary family. The emphasis was on the possessive—teaching students to use the 's inflectional morpheme, as in *José is Silvia's son*. The lesson also practiced using the possessive adjectives, as in *José is her son* or *Her son is José*. There were many exercises around this fictional family, yet such fictional families are not meaningful to the students. After MALP training, Mr. Thomas designed a project whereby the students brought photos or made drawings of their own families and created collages with the relevant sentences about their actual families. Then they were able to practice asking each other questions and answering them using real information. Some students even discovered they knew some family members of their fellow students, which, in turn, helped build interconnectedness that was not possible using the textbook exclusively. Thus, a MALP project can enhance textbook lessons by applying the material to students' lives in meaningful ways.

Crossing the Mekong: A Shared Experience

We conclude the chapter on designing MALP projects by referring again to the MALP Checklist. Earlier we considered how Mrs. Jansson referred to the MALP chart and Checklist to ensure incorporating all the elements of MALP. This section examines in greater detail how another teacher, Mrs. Cicero, incorporated all six elements of MALP into a MALP project.

Refugees from a particular area, ethnic group, or country often have shared experiences leading to their arrival in their new homeland. Mrs. Cicero's class initiated a MALP project based on her students' shared experiences as Hmong refugees during the period 1975–1990. Her Crossing the Mekong Project closely linked to the students' backgrounds. This project arose because Mrs. Cicero learned about her students' history and found a common experience, that of crossing the Mekong River to escape from Laos to Thailand. She decided this could be used to generate a MALP project. Like Mrs. Janssen's birthday project, this one included learning about dates, but from a very different perspective. The Hmong came from the highlands of Laos, fleeing life-threatening conditions they faced there as a result of having helped the United States during the Vietnam War. After 1975, crossing the Mekong River, they arrived in Thailand and from there went on to other countries, such as the United States.

Mrs. Cicero guided the beginning-level adults as they conducted a survey of how each of them had crossed the Mekong River. Crossing the Mekong was a very significant event in the Hmong saga, one that is commemorated in their art and described in their storytelling. Figure 5.1 recreates the chalkboard in the classroom on which Mrs. Cicero developed this activity. It should be pointed out that the students' memories and recollections of their crossing were often vague and, that to complete this survey, the students had to talk with family members, locate documents, and recover the details of their experience as refugees. In this survey, adults with little or no prior literacy or educational background participated in generating a chart and using flags, pictures, names, numbers, and a few key vocabulary words

FIGURE 5.1 Chalkboard Diagram

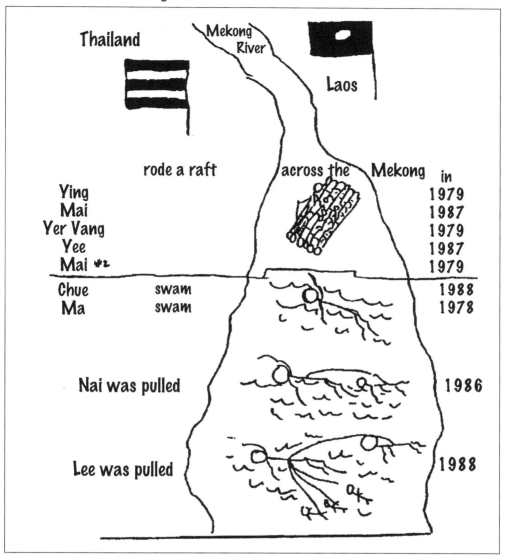

to present their data. Moreover, the chalkboard in Mrs. Cicero's classroom mirrored their artwork, *paj ntaub*, in which they showed through this medium the story of their journey from Laos to Thailand. An example of a *paj ntaub* can be seen at www.sciencebuzz.org/museum/object/2004_08_hmong_story_cloth.

Using the MALP Checklist with a Sample Project

MALP project–based learning differs in an essential way from other project-based learning in that teachers refer to the Checklist introduced in Chapter 3 at each stage to insure that they are incorporating the six elements of MALP along the way. The use of the MALP checklist for project planning, implementation, and evaluation will become evident as projects are described and discussed.

Using the MALP checklist, let's analyze the Mekong activity to see how Mrs. Cicero succeeded in designing and implementing a MALP project (see Figure 5.2).

It should be evident through Mrs. Cicero's project how the application of MALP through this kind of activity helps struggling L2 learners make the learning paradigm shift. A MALP project transitions learners to participation and success in formal education. It accepts the two conditions for learning, makes transitions to individual achievement and the written word comfortably, and teaches academic ways of thinking. Pivotal to MALP is that the projects are not isolated from the students' world outside the classroom where they are created. This experientially constructed view of reality invites and enhances active learning.

FIGURE 5.2 Mrs. Cicero's Completed MALP Checklist

Mutually Adaptive Learning Paradigm – MALP
Teacher Planning Checklist

A. Accept Conditions for Learning

A1. I am making this lesson/project immediately relevant to my students. ☐
The students are describing an important event in their lives and learning how to read and write about it in English. They are talking with their families about shared, meaningful, and valuable experiences.

A2. I am helping students develop and maintain interconnectedness. ☐
Students share their personal experiences with each other and share them with their teacher, so that their relationships grow and strengthen.

B. Combine Processes for Learning

B1. I am incorporating both shared responsibility and individual accountability. ☐
The individuals provided their own data for the activity and the class as a whole worked together on recording it and illustrating it.

B2. I am scaffolding the written word through oral interaction. ☐
The data was collected orally at home and shared orally in class. The teacher wrote as the students shared the ways they crossed the river and the dates. Then the class read from the board and finally, they wrote their own data down in their notebooks.

C. Focus on New Activities for Learning

C1. I am focusing on tasks requiring academic ways of thinking. ☐
The teacher asked the students questions about the data on the board. Some of the questions she asked were: How many different ways did the students cross the Mekong? What was the most common way the students in the class crossed the river? What was the earliest year students crossed the Mekong? The latest year? What year did the most people in the class cross the river? These questions encouraged them to look at more than their own personal experience and showed them how to look at a set of information and draw conclusions from it.

C2. I am making these tasks accessible to my students with familiar language
and content. ☐
The content for the project came from their personal experience, so it was not unfamiliar to them. Students collected the data about their experience in the native language from their family members. When they shared this information in English, the language consisted of words they were familiar with or learned very naturally because of their own personal experiences. The teacher asked questions that required short responses using the words from the board.

6

Flipping the Classroom

Ms. Bronsen delivered a lesson about using context clues to guess the meaning of an unfamiliar word. She used the think-aloud technique to question each part of the sentence to demonstrate how she could apply what she knew to understand the new word. After she modeled the context clue activity, she introduced a second unfamiliar word and, step-by-step, revealed her analysis of the new word, pausing for students to think and try their own responses. Finally, she introduced a challenge activity for the students to think about and then asked them to bring their ideas to the next class to share.

At first glance, Ms. Bronsen presented a traditional lesson. However, just the opposite was true. Rather than presenting this lesson during class time, she videotaped it and had her students view it on their own time before the class convened. The challenge she presented in the video lesson was the first activity taken up when the class met together; it was completed in small groups as Ms. Bronsen circulated, assisting students as needed. What this teacher did was to "flip her classroom." This approach to teaching has been referred to using various terms, such as *inverse teaching* (Lage, Platt, & Treglia, 2000) or *peer instruction* (Mazur, 1997). The most common term, popularized in large part by the work of Jonathan Bergmann and Aaron Sams (2009), is the *flipped classroom*.

This chapter shows that this technique responds to the interactive needs of struggling L2 learners, who are least likely to take advantage of the opportunities provided by the question-and-answer sequences used in traditional lesson formats. Instead, these learners need a lesson delivery model that increases their chances of classroom participation and mastery of material.

Typical Classroom Interaction—IRE/IRF

The typical question-and-answer exchange found in Western-style classrooms consists of a teacher posing a question, a student responding to the question, and then an evaluation of the response by the teacher (see, e.g., Abd-Kadir & Hardman, 2007; Bearne, 1999; Cazden, 1988, 2001; Pontefract & Hardman, 2005; Vaish, 2008).

EXAMPLE 1

Mrs. Schwartz:	What is Boyle's Law?
Janine:	Pressure is inversely proportional to volume.
Mrs. Schwartz:	Good.
Mrs. Schwartz:	What is the formula for Boyle's Law?
Janine:	PV = k
Mrs. Schwartz:	Excellent. So now, we can take an example and solve it.

During this cycle, the other students are expected to sit and listen quietly while the teacher talks, speaking only when called upon (Gay, 2000). This pattern is known as Initiation-Response-Evaluation or IRE (Mehan, 1979; Sinclair & Coulthard, 1975). Researchers often refer to the questions posed as part of this pattern as *display questions* because they merely ask students to recall previously transmitted knowledge and/or knowledge obvious to all. This three-part sequence creates minimal opportunities for student participation and encourages little, if any, critical thinking (Cazden, 1988).

The IRF (Initiation-Response-Feedback) pattern, an enhanced version of the IRE, also requires a display of mastered knowledge. However, rather than focusing solely on the accuracy of the response, the teacher provides additional feedback to students (Wells, 1993).

EXAMPLE 2

Mrs. Schwartz:	Who knows what Boyle's Law is?
Aisha:	(Raising her hand and saying:) I do, I do.
Mrs. Schwartz:	Okay Aisha, why don't you tell us about Boyle's Law?
Aisha:	It shows how pressure changes when volume changes.
Mrs. Schwartz:	Yes, and we now can look at how pressure changes. Can you share with us what happens to pressure when the volume gets higher?

Aisha:	It goes down.
Mrs. Schwartz:	Yes, tell me more about that.
Aisha:	Pressure decreases when volume increases.
Mrs. Schwartz:	. . . and we will see that pressure and volume are inversely proportional. Here is a problem we can solve together.

In the IRF sequence, providing the response is only the beginning of an interaction as instructors follow up with a *why?* or *how?* probe for the type of response that makes the underlying thinking transparent. When Mrs. Schwartz asks, "Can you share with us what happens to pressure when the volume gets higher?" followed by "Tell me more about that," we see that the interaction continues like a guided conversation. Here Aisha does not see her answer as an end-point, but rather as a link in a communicative chain or *uptake*, a teacher's use of a student response to extend the dialogue (Nystrand et al., 2003). Through uptake, students engage more successfully with the content and take greater ownership of new information (Tharpe & Gallimore, 1991). Uptake is highly valued as a means of having students engage in academic discourse and academic ways of thinking. For many ELLs, this type of conversational engagement alone can make a significant difference in that such exchanges result in meaningful communication (Toohey, Waterstone, & Julé-Lemke, 2000).

For struggling L2 learners, these practices, while good, are not sufficient. When teachers use unfamiliar questioning strategies, there is little or no active participation (Luk & Lin, 2007; Wiltse, 2006). These students are not yet at the point where they can engage in academic ways of thinking without appropriate scaffolding. As a result, they may be reluctant to volunteer any thoughts or questions about the content on their own; additionally, their cultural practices may further prohibit them from questioning authority, in this case the teacher (Pon, Goldstein, & Schecter, 2003; Townsend & Fu, 2001).

Moreover, as discussed in earlier chapters, struggling L2 learners generally range on the left end of the Ways of Learning Continuum and come from backgrounds where communication is generally seen as something used to carry out a pragmatic task or activity (Paradise & Rogoff, 2009). Talk between adults and children takes place in order to share necessary information rather than to express or display knowledge, the didactics of the Western-style classroom (Ochs & Schiefflin, 1985; Rogoff et al., 2007). Indeed, as Walsh (2011), points out, the IRE/IRF sequence in the sense of the teacher (or "questioner") assessing student knowledge and/or comprehension, is not found outside the classroom and certainly is not part of informal ways of learning. Moreover, even those who have participated in formal education may be accustomed to classroom settings that rely principally, or even exclusively, on memorization and recitation, with a minimum, if any, student-initiated talk. In short, the characteristic IRE/IRF question-and-answer sequences do not meet the needs of the struggling L2 learners discussed in this book.

"Flipping" the Classroom

The basic flipped classroom model centers around two essential components: out-of-class direct instruction and in-class application of material. The direct instruction is delivered by teachers via pre-recorded video lessons outside the classroom. Class time is used to engage the students in activities designed to apply the concepts and language introduced via video. This style flips what is traditionally done in the classroom with what is traditionally done outside the classroom. It turns teaching "inside out" by having the lesson concept presentation take place **outside** of the classroom and the home assignments take place **inside** the classroom (Bergmann & Sams, 2009), hence the term *flipped*.

As shown in the discussion of IRE and IRF interactions, the teacher is the central figure in initiating and controlling student interaction in most classrooms. However, in the flipped classroom, as Alison King is often quoted as saying, the teacher is no longer the "sage on the stage"; the teacher becomes the "guide on the side" (King, 1993). Because the direct instruction occurs outside of class, the teacher no longer needs to focus primarily on presenting information during class time. The teacher's role in the flipped classroom is to provide guidance in helping students extract and process information, gain skills, and develop language proficiency.

When teachers become facilitators of learning, they are no longer the central figure, classroom authority, and transmitter of knowledge. Learning becomes active rather than passive since students become dynamically engaged in their own learning process through various classroom activities (Cherney, 2008; Fredericks, Blumenfeld, & Paris, 2004). The flipped classroom can thus be seen as another step in the mutual adaptation process in transitioning struggling L2 learners to Western-style formal education.

Bloom's Taxonomy and Flipped Learning

Bloom's Taxonomy (Bloom 1956; revised Anderson & Krathwohl, 2001) is useful in examining what happens in flipped learning. In a traditional classroom setting, struggling L2 learners put most of their effort into the lower levels of the taxonomy, understanding and remembering, as they attempt to follow teacher's instructional delivery. In the flipped classroom, the teacher moves these lower levels of the taxonomy to outside of the class where students work on mastering concepts on their own time and at their own pace. They can pause, rewind the recording, or review the lesson at any time. In class, the teacher and students focus on the upper levels of the taxonomy, applying, analyzing, and creating. This allows struggling L2 learners more opportunities to understand and remember before they come to class and have to keep up with other students in their classes who have stronger educational and literacy backgrounds. Bloom's taxonomy itself is flipped, or inverted, with lower levels addressed in the video lessons and the upper levels developed in the classroom.

As shown in Chapter 4, academic ways of thinking and, by extension, decontextualized tasks, are a challenge for struggling L2 learners. In flipped learning, these tasks are undertaken in class, with peer and teacher support readily available. The flipped classroom places responsibility on the students to manage learning, which results in the development of higher-order thinking skills. Because the students are the ones who are making connections between the lesson delivered outside the classroom and the activities in the classroom, they are engaging in synthesis and application. At the same time, since class time is used for activities and projects, learning becomes a shared experience and a group exploration time so that the students challenge each other to develop higher levels of thinking.

The Science Lesson

Mrs. Schwartz's Videos

In the section on IRE/IRF, we observed Mrs. Schwartz introducing Boyle's Law. Let's return to her lesson and see how Mrs. Schwartz, now trained in flipped learning techniques, presents this concept.

In her first video lesson, Mrs. Schwartz begins by demonstrating and describing examples of Boyle's Law in ways and with language familiar to the students, by tailoring the vocabulary and questions for the students. Before recording the lesson, she has prepared a slide presentation with keywords, such as *higher/lower* and *increase/decrease*. In the video, she introduces, and repeats several times, the sentence pattern *When X goes up, Y goes down.*

Her initial task is to convey the concept of an inverse proportion. In her video, Mrs. Schwartz gives an example that may resonate with some learners. She wants students to learn that, for a given distance, the faster one goes, the less time it takes to get there, so speed is inversely proportional to time.

Mrs. Schwartz tries to make the topic relevant by setting her example in the local community and talking about how fast a car goes.

EXAMPLE 3

Mrs. Schwartz: Javier is driving to work today and he is late. The speed limit is 30 miles per hour, but he decides to go faster today and hopes nobody sees that. Why does he want to go faster than the speed limit? Think about that. (*pauses and changes slide*)

She then provides a problem with numbers

Mrs. Schwartz: If he goes 30 miles per hour for 15 minutes to work, he will be late. If he goes 37 miles per hour, he will be on time. Will it take less time or more time when he goes faster? (*pauses and changes slide*)

Mrs. Schwartz: So if the speed is higher, it takes less time to drive the same distance. This is called *inverse proportion*. The more something goes up, like Javier's speed, the more something else goes down, like the time it takes Javier. If Javier drives less than the speed limit, which is 30 miles per hour, will he get to work earlier or later? We can say that when X goes up, or increases, Y goes down, or decreases. This is an example of an inverse proportion.

This video lesson has three components:

- Vocabulary: *increase, decrease, inverse proportion*
- Grammar: expressions of comparison/contrast—*more, less, less than, -er (higher, faster), the more . . . the more*
- Content: concept of an inverse relationship between two factors that affect each other.

Mrs. Schwartz scaffolds all three lesson components by guiding the students' learning in the video lessons she prepares. She makes several videos, each with a different and more challenging example, to make the material manageable for her students. She moves from using basic language to more complex vocabulary; from an everyday example to a more scientific one. Finally, she engages the students in questions requiring individual analysis and evaluation. Mrs. Schwartz provides a meaningful and relevant context that students can view and review on their own as often as they like. She asks key questions and provides vocabulary, visuals, and sentence frames.

In her next video, Mrs. Schwartz introduces the scientific perspective to help students understand Boyle's Law. She first describes an everyday example of gas and volume and the squeezing of a balloon. When squeezing a balloon, the volume of the gas inside is reduced, which increases the pressure. Since the balloon cannot withstand the added pressure, it bursts. In her video lesson, Mrs. Schwartz demonstrates this happening.

For the second example, a more scientific one but one still likely to be familiar, Mrs. Schwartz presents the topic "change of pressure in a syringe" and shares this information:

> A syringe is an everyday device used to draw blood samples or give injections. When the plunger of the syringe is pulled back, the volume inside the syringe increases, decreasing the pressure. To balance this effect of low pressure, air or blood is sucked in through the needle, thus equalizing the pressure inside and outside the container.

As she speaks, she uses a syringe filled with cranberry juice to illustrate the points she is making.

Mrs. Schwartz next uses the screen-sharing feature to show the class a website, www.grc.nasa.gov/WWW/k-12/airplane/aboyle.html. On this website, they can see an animated schematic depicting how the change in the pressure exerted on a gas can reduce the space it occupies. She has moved the students from on-camera demonstrations to a more abstract depiction of the concept, albeit one that is visual. The visual includes dials that show pressure changing, while mass and temperature remain constant. It shows how adding or removing weights to a piston positioned above the container of gas changes the pressure and, inversely, the volume, of the gas itself. Accompanying this schematic is a basic graph, showing the volume on the y-axis and the pressure on the x-axis, with the curve on the graph moving along as the animation illustrates Boyle's Law. Using her mouse pointer, Mrs. Schwartz calls attention to each element of the schematic in turn. In this example, she uses the scientific language associated with Boyle's Law, along with appropriate sentence frames to scaffold her oral presentation of the concept. Her final video lesson on Boyle's Law shows the formula, $PV = k$, where k represents a constant and introduces the terms *pounds per square inch (psi)* for pressure and *liter (l)* for volume, giving her students the mathematical symbols and units of measure they will need for solving problems in class.

At the conclusion of each video lesson, Mrs. Schwartz asks the students to think about the information she presented and to be ready to talk about it in class, where they will apply their new learning about inverse proportions of volume and pressure and Boyle's Law. She also invites her students to bring their own examples of the concept presented and be ready to share them with the group.

The purpose of these videos is to prepare the students for class by giving them information and examples to examine and consider without a solution. This process is the foundation for scaffolding the new concept: inverse proportionality.

Mrs. Schwartz's Classroom Activities

Once students have watched Mrs. Schwartz's pre-recorded video lessons on inverse proportion and Boyle's Law, they come to class ready for activities. In her first activity, *molecules* (Armstrong, 2009), students become "molecules" of air in a "container;" that is, moving around in a clearly defined corner of the classroom. Mrs. Schwartz instructs the students to move about in this area. Two students are given a length of yarn to hold. Each of them takes one end of the yarn and together they start walking closer to the "molecules." The size of the "container" gradually reduces as the two students holding the yarn close in on the "molecules," causing them to increasingly bump into one another. In this way, the class experiences together what they viewed at home—that is, the smaller the space, the more pressure there is, and the greater the space, the less pressure. This is a kinesthetic representation of the key concept underlying Boyle's Law that Mrs. Schwartz presented in the video lessons.

In subsequent activities, Mrs. Schwartz has the students work collaboratively to accomplish these tasks, each one based on one of the three schemata outlined in Chapter 2: the formal schema, the content schema, and the linguistic schema:

- show their understanding of the concept of inverse proportions (formal schema, that is, engage in a new way of thinking)
- apply the concept to Boyle's Law—that is, the relationship between pressure and volume of a gas (content schema—science)
- solve problems describing actual situations using Boyle's Law (linguistic schema—complex language of word problems)

For each task, Mrs. Schwartz provides students with different options. For the first task, they can illustrate examples of items that are in inverse proportion to each other by:

- making a storyboard based on the example from the video about Javier getting to work. Their example should show two people, one driving slowly and one driving faster, indicating the time it took them each to go the same distance, to illustrate the concept that the faster one moves, the less time is required, or

- creating a series of pictures depicting the kinesthetic activity, showing the space between the "molecules" decreasing as the two students holding the length of yarn close in.

For the second task, the students can show by different means that they understood how inverse proportion applies to pressure and volume. In order of difficulty, these are:

- creating a poster with the syringe example from their teacher's video, with a description explaining what happens when the syringe is depressed

- making a screenshot of the animated schematic from the NASA website they viewed in Mrs. Schwartz's video lesson, inserting labels for the items shown, and adding a caption

- preparing their own video showing how Boyle's Law works by demonstrating and describing the balloon example.

Finally they are ready for the third task, looking at word problems. This final task is particularly important as this is how students are assessed on standardized tests. The class collaborates in identifying the elements of the problems and uses their knowledge of Boyle's Law to figure out how to set up the problem from the language provided. They now have both an understanding of the concept and a familiarity with the vocabulary to complete a problem such as:

A tank has 8 liters of gas under 14 pounds per square inch of pressure. When the pressure increases to 28 pounds per square inch, what will the volume of the gas become?

To solve it, they will use the formula for Boyle's Law: $PV = k$. Only now, when they have mastered the underlying concepts and the language for the problems, does Mrs. Schwartz present the word problem. To support them, she puts up a poster illustrating the inverse relationship by writing the letters in dif-

FIGURE 6.1 Visual Representation of the Inverse Proportionality of Pressure and Volume

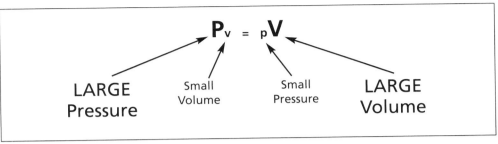

From Hewitt, 2011, Slide 15.

ferent sizes, using *p* for pressure and *v* for volume, as shown in Figure 6.1 (Hewitt, 2011). In this way, Mrs. Schwartz connects the concept to the mathematical symbols.

In small groups, the students solve word problems using the formula for Boyle's Law. Then they work individually, showing their work to fellow students and the teacher for feedback. As they tackle the problems, their teacher provides clarification as needed. Mrs. Schwartz's struggling L2 learners are succeeding in mastering this material through the flipped learning approach.

Benefits of Flipping the MALP Classroom

Many of the features of the flipped classroom model provide valuable enhancements to the MALP instructional model. When conducted with struggling L2 learners in mind, both the pre-recorded video lessons and the classroom activities and interactions reinforce the elements of MALP.

Video Lessons

Videos are an excellent way to clarify new concepts with visual and interactive support from the teacher by incorporating appropriate redundancy, and other devices used in oral transmission of learning, as described earlier. Comprehension increases as students can view these video lessons on demand, enabling them to learn at their own pace and within their own timeframe. The increase in comprehensibility for struggling L2 learners, especially those who prefer oral transmission, emerges from the ability to be taught by the teacher orally at home and to control the oral transmission with pauses, repetition, and individually guided questions to think about and prepare for class. The recorded interactive presentation, including the accompanying guide questions, provides students with the reinforcement that they require—something that is difficult to get in a traditional classroom. Together with the classroom activities, video lessons help transition struggling L2 learners to the use of print for accessing and transmitting information, an essential element of MALP.

For struggling L2 learners, and in keeping with the MALP model, the video lesson presentations and demonstrations should be prepared and recorded by the students' teacher and not by another instructor. The videos are not merely lectures; they are virtual classrooms, where the relationship with the teacher is still key. This use of technology supports student learning by providing increased opportunities for comprehensible input, carefully selected for them by their teacher, and individually controlled by students themselves. Moreover, because their virtual classroom is always available, they can make connections with the material and with their teacher, whether or not they are able to attend the physical class.

In a MALP-based flipped classroom, the computer screen is laid out similar to what is shown in Figure 6.2. There are three sections visible on the screen: a webcam, a list of guide questions, and a main section for a slide presentation or screen-sharing options for other applications and/or websites. Using the webcam, teachers employ gestures, facial expressions, and other non-verbal cues while recording the video lesson. The guide questions appear below the webcam and next to the presentation. This ensures that students see listed what

FIGURE 6.2 Sample Screenshot of Video Lesson

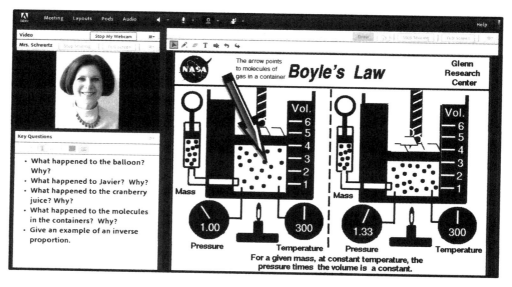

they are expected to understand and remember from the video lesson so that they can participate in the subsequent in-class activities. The questions chosen to guide students' learning mirror the ways of thinking required for the tasks students will perform in the classroom following the lesson.

The main section of the screen usually includes a set of slides along with documents, websites, videos, and other relevant material teachers share to illustrate and clarify essential points. During the recorded lesson, the teacher inserts think-alouds along the way, a technique in which students are guided to articulate their thoughts as they read or encounter new material. This technique encourages struggling L2 learners to become explicitly aware of what strategies they are using to process and understand the information they are encountering (Chamot & O'Malley, 1994). Throughout the video lesson, teachers provide scaffolding for the new content and language by showing students how to construct meaning for unfamiliar vocabulary, creating analogies, demonstrating how to use graphic organizers and other visuals, and/or making connections to prior knowledge (Jiménez, Garcia, & Pearson, 1996; Wade, 1990).

As the lesson proceeds, teachers reveal information and questions on the slides. There are frequent pauses in the delivery while teachers ask students to reflect on a point, answer questions, or analyze information. Only then do they move on with the lesson, revealing the next bit of information or the answer to a previously posed question. This technique mirrors the familiar mode of oral transmission and keeps the lesson interactive, even though it is pre-recorded. Students can even, and do, ask family and friends to join them as they view the lesson, making the flipped classroom a way to connect and deepen the relationship between the teacher, the students, the classroom and the school experience. Nola, for example, watched video lessons with her boyfriend. Answering the questions became a game as they both shouted out answers. Thus, this approach also strengthens the home-school connection.

Providing lessons through online video tools allows for a mobile learning environment where students can access lessons from school or home computers, on DVDs or the internet, or from smartphones, tablets, or online-stored resources. Struggling L2 learners often have attendance issues, and miss classroom instruction (Marshall, DeCapua, & Antolini, 2010; Martínez, 2009). In traditional classrooms, gaps in learning due to absence are not easily filled. The flipped classroom model provides an alternative way to access lessons. Because students can view the pre-recorded video lessons at any time, and even more than once, they never miss essential material. Furthermore, such continual access also allows students to feel a part of the learning community of the classroom.

The technology used for the pre-recorded video portion of the flipped classroom model can take many forms. There is specifically designed software, such as Camtasia, or many other readily available and easy-to-use alternatives. The flipped classroom, although ideally used with the internet, is not dependent on it. If the internet is unavailable or slow, videos can be loaded onto a USB drive, tablet, smartphone, or placed on a DVD. As new technology emerges, the flipped classroom can be adapted accordingly, as long as the pedagogical principles are consistent with the MALP instructional model.

Classroom Activities and Interaction

The video lessons themselves are a powerful means for teachers to reach struggling L2 learners; however, the most important question to consider when flipping a MALP classroom is how the class time will be spent. Fostering active learning in the class is the key to effective flipped learning. With direct instruction taking place outside of class, time in class consists of:

- clarifying remaining confusion or misconceptions about material presented in the videos
- engaging the students in activities that apply the concepts from the videos
- observing students closely to ensure on-task attention and equal participation of all learners
- assessing how well each student is doing with the content, based on contributions, questions, and involvement
- encouraging the building of higher-level thinking skills.

From the very beginning of the class, students are meaningfully involved in learning, as in Mrs. Schwartz's molecules activity, which reinforced Boyle's Law using familiar language and content. Moreover, the flipped classroom also presents greater opportunities for peer instruction since there are continually ways for students to share responsibility for their knowledge and understanding.

In the flipped classroom, learning becomes truly interactive as students engage with the material and with each other. When communication is ongoing, and not closed-ended as in the cyclical IRE/IRF teacher-student patterns, students feel better able to contribute and to pose questions. This process, however, does not occur automatically. Active participation skills must be nurtured. Merely putting students into small groups does not address the issue of how to promote active student participation (Wiltse, 2006). Students accustomed to informal discussions with peers may not know how to engage in classroom discussions.

Many struggling L2 learners come from cultures that view the teacher as an authority figure who controls the classroom and interactions and may not feel comfortable initially with ongoing two-way communication. For some students, especially those from highly collectivistic cultures, speaking up in class may run counter to their notions of viewing the class as a whole so that such action may be seen as disruptive rather than participatory (Watkins, 2000). In addition, like many L2 learners, they may feel hesitant to participate because of their lack of language proficiency (Mohr & Mohr, 2007). Since one principle of the ICF (see Chapter 2) is an emphasis on relationships, teachers strive to address and mitigate students' reluctance to participate, regardless of the reason. They can do so by nurturing a sense of community in the classroom, one in which teacher-student and student-student interaction is valued and necessary, which then results in more communication and greater opportunity for increasing L2 language proficiency.

Mrs. Navarro's Flipped MALP Classroom

We have explored how the flipped classroom, with its combination of pre-recorded video lessons and carefully structured, dynamic, cognitively demanding, in-class collaborative activities supports struggling L2 learners, promotes their success in Western-style learning settings and is consistent with the MALP instructional model.

Let's take a look at Mrs. Navarro's flipped classroom through the lens of the MALP Checklist. Mrs. Navarro teaches a low-proficiency group of L2 learners in an adult education program. Many of the students have expressed an interest in learning more about banks and banking. Some of the students are familiar with this in their own countries but not in the United States; others know about the general concept of banks but have never used one (*immediate relevance*).

In her videos, Mrs. Navarro uses basic language, introduces key phrases, and has questions for the students in a sidebar as she talks about banking. To keep the material manageable for these students, she keeps the videos short and focuses on one item at a time.

In the first video lesson on banking, Mrs. Navarro shows the students some banks in the neighborhood, the ATM machines, and images of ATM cards, as well as checkbooks and checks. In the second video, she shows a brief animated presentation from the web on using an ATM machine. In the third video, she shows a clip of someone opening a bank account.[1] In the fourth and final video, she demonstrates how to write a check.

In class, Mrs. Navarro provides not only "traditional" banking activities but also other activities to help the students learn broader concepts that they will need for banking. In groups, the students make charts of various banking activities such as the steps for using an ATM, the parts of a check, and opening up a bank account (*interconnectedness, decontextualized task*).

To practice numbers, the students play Bingo; however, rather than Mrs. Navarro providing them with the game, the students in groups make different Bingo games by thinking of numbers to use (*interconnectedness*). Mrs. Navarro encourages the groups to use numbers important to them, such as birth year, favorite number, house numbers, bus numbers, ages of family members, the address of the school building, and so on (*immediate relevance*). The groups then take turns in leading the game and practicing numbers (*oral to print*).

During another activity, Mrs. Navarro has the students draw numbers from a hat, say the number, and then take an index card and write that number (*oral to print*). If Magda draws 27, then she writes twenty-seven; if Hector draws 450, he writes four hundred and fifty. This activity provides the students with practice that will help them in check writing (*decontextualized task*). After all the students have practiced writing their numbers on their cards, the students have to order the numbers from lowest to highest (*decontextualized task*), reading and saying each number (*print to oral*). As a follow-up, Mrs. Navarro asks the students to choose banking activity based on one of the charts the different groups have prepared, go out into the real world, and report back to the class. Alternatively, for those reluctant or unable to actually do so, she suggests that they describe what one of their family members or friends did (*interconnectedness, immediate relevance*).

In this chapter, we have seen how teachers can enhance the MALP instructional model by incorporating the flipped classroom. The flipped learning approach combined with MALP creates a stronger learning community. It provides the necessary climate for meaningful communication, supportive and non-judgmental teachers and classmates, timely and useful feedback, and cognitive engagement that will result in students' retention and mastery of new concepts and skills as they move along the Ways of Learning Continuum (Ruus et

---

[1] Although we have previously emphasized the importance of teacher-made videos, at times the teacher will need to use other resources for security or legal reasons.

al., 2007). In sum, the flipped classroom is a way to scaffold students into Western-style learning.

Designing instruction for struggling L2 learners is a major part of a MALP approach; however, if teachers are not cognizant of the interplay of all elements that need to be present in a MALP classroom, they may fall short of a full implementation of the model. As teachers implement MALP, the classroom itself takes on a new look and feel. A MALP classroom includes the physical environment as well as the interactional dynamics among the students and teacher. The next chapter examines a MALP classroom to see what it looks like when this type of instruction is taking place.

7

The MALP Learning Environment

Entering a MALP classroom, one immediately sees evidence of a dynamic space filled with student-produced materials. The students have brought in or developed collaboratively in class, many items reflecting what they are learning and sharing with each other and their teacher. Here we look at two classrooms—Mrs. Suoto's ESL mathematics class and Mrs. Mochak's ESL adult literacy class—to examine how the physical setting evolved as they implemented the MALP model.

Mrs. Suoto and Mrs. Mochak have also "flipped" their instruction, as outlined in the previous chapter. This flipping has made the focus of filling the classroom with student-produced materials much smoother and faster, as the students get ideas and suggestions from their teacher about what they can bring with them to class as examples of what they saw in the video lessons. They also regularly create materials in class that illustrate what the videos taught them.

When we first entered Mrs. Suoto's ESL mathematics class, we noticed the relatively bare walls. There were a few commercially prepared posters of the alphabet and people reading books; there was a world map and some flags from the students' home countries. Her class was comprised of struggling L2 learners, many of whom were clearly frustrated and resentful about having to be in an ESL classroom.

Mrs. Mochak's adult education class took place in a small room that was crowded with cubicles for books, bookshelves, wood paneling, and glass walls facing the hallway. The students were day workers and young mothers. Attendance was sporadic depending on work and family responsibilities. After both classrooms underwent a MALP intervention, they were very different places.

As Mrs. Suoto and Mrs. Mochak learned more about MALP, their rooms began to change. With every visit to each classroom, we noted more student-produced items on the walls and more fluidity in their room arrangements (how furniture was arranged), which led to a stronger sense that the class owned the room. Each classroom gradually became the students' space and better represented them and what they were learning. In each case, we can clearly see the many ways in which a supportive learning setting is evident. Much of the basis for interconnectedness and the scaffolding for academic ways of thinking are provided through students' choices of materials and activities placed around the classroom. From the calendar to the word wall, the seating arrangements to the resource center, students were now surrounded by support and materials to assist them in their learning. The stage is now set for dynamic lessons that are complemented by the physical setting. For example, in Mrs. Mochak's class after she transitioned to a MALP classroom, we found:

> brightly colored posters illustrating key concepts covering the walls that had been created by the students during class in a collaborative learning community. The students were applying concepts they had learned in the interactive video lecture. The students were each responsible for a root word they were presenting to the group. The assignment was to detail as many forms and uses for the word as possible. The students taught one another about their words while the teacher stood at the back of the class, gently coaching but not inhibiting interactions.

The Classroom

The ideal MALP classroom is similar to what many would think of as an elementary classroom but with age-appropriate modifications. The walls of a MALP classroom display materials prepared by students, teachers, and others. These include a class calendar, posters and murals, and other language-related material.

Class Calendar

The calendar is an anchor point for the class. Its value extends far beyond the basic role of recording information by date. Adhering to the school and class is often a challenge for struggling L2 learners. Careful attention to clock time and time management is less common in many cultures, whether due to different priorities, an agrarian environment dependent on solar and climate factors, or other causes (Hall, 1966). To help transition struggling L2 learners to more

Western-style notions of time and scheduling, the teacher can establish a class calendar. The calendar is where the students check upcoming events, assignments, and due dates, as well as share personal information such as birthdays and family weddings. Because the students actively contribute to its content, the calendar builds a sense of ownership. The calendar fosters interconnectedness because it includes not only school and class information, but also special events in students' lives.

In Mrs. Suoto's classroom, our attention is immediately drawn to the classroom calendar filled with information. Each day the students review what is listed on the calendar for the day. At the close of class, Mrs. Suoto or a student formally crosses off the day, and the students together preview the next day and the next week to see what is ahead. Mrs. Suoto refers to previous days and weeks to remind students of what they have done together. The calendar provides opportunities for practicing authentic uses for the various verb tenses as students discuss what they have done, are doing, and will do on specific dates. All these steps help struggling L2 learners with scheduling and planning and supports conditions for learning, interconnectedness, and immediate relevance.

Concept Posters

Teachers are familiar with graphic organizers that visually present knowledge, concepts, or ideas. The ideal MALP classroom goes beyond graphic organizers to incorporate concept posters. Concept posters are specifically created by teachers and students to support what the students are learning and are visualizations of essential ideas that underpin the specific information to be discussed, processed, and/or written in class. A MALP classroom displays concept posters that serve as references and guides for students in terms of academic ways of thinking.

Mrs. Suoto made extensive use of concept posters. At one point when her students were learning about geometric shapes, Mrs. Suoto created a poster with a large right triangle with the three sides labeled: horizontal, vertical, and diagonal. Next to each side, she listed real-world objects to help students understand how the new concept of a right triangle is related to things familiar to them. For horizontal, she wrote *shadow, ground, floor,* and *path*; for vertical, *building, tree, pole, person,* and *lighthouse*; and for diagonal, *ladder, wire, kite string,* and *hill*. This concept poster aided the students in conceptualizing and visualizing a right triangle.

Student-made posters provide instant reminders and constantly available resources to support academic ways of thinking and demonstrate internalization of the content. Such concept posters are collaborative and individual efforts that engage students and foster the transition from the oral to the written.

The Wonder Wall

An innovation in Mrs. Suoto's class prompted by her MALP training was her Wonder Wall. This is a designated bulletin board or a large sheet of paper taped to the wall where students post questions and items of interest related to the course material and where other students read and reply or comment. Students may bring in questions that have arisen from the flipped classroom videos, from class activities, from readings, or from their personal experiences. They peruse the questions other students have posed, take time to think about them, and post a response, additional comment, or another question. One of Mrs. Suoto's students posted a photo of a yield sign and the question, "Shape?" Another student wrote the word *triangle* beneath it. Interactions like this promote language use without pressure to perform and encourage students to actively engage the material without their teacher as the intermediary.

The Wonder Wall extends MALP and creates an interactive, student-constructed space based on the written word. Students read their fellow students' contributions, sharing and discussing what they have found on the Wonder Wall and getting ideas for additional material to place there. To participate, students need to read and write, further developing their connection to print. The teacher periodically checks the Wonder Wall to observe the students' thinking and address any misconceptions or queries that require clarification.

If the teacher is using the flipped learning approach, the Wonder Wall becomes part of the in-class collaboration generated by the direct instruction from the video lessons. Following the Boyle's Law lesson in Ms. Schwartz's class, one student found and posted information about Robert Boyle, who first demonstrated the phenomenon in 1662. Another student put up a series of photos of herself filling both cheeks with air and then forcing the air from one cheek to the other. She wrote beneath the photos: *Is this a good example of Boyle's Law?* Once the students sense that this is truly their space, it becomes an opportunity for peer teaching and a deepening sense of interconnectedness.

Murals

Mural creation fosters ownership, an important dimension in learning. Murals are public art and say something about the community of learners who create them—who they are, what they think, what's important to them. Because murals are primarily visual with some key words and phrases, they say these things in ways all viewers can understand and appreciate. Murals often illus-trate the hopes, values, and priorities of the learning community. They can represent what the learners feel is important about their past, which sometimes includes images of places that no longer exist. Murals can also commemorate significant people or pivotal events in the lives of the students. As such, murals exemplify the MALP instructional model.

Mrs. Mochak's students generally congregated outside a long hallway connecting the different classrooms, chatting with each other before and after class. Reflecting on ways to capitalize on their behavior and include the elements of MALP, she decided to have her class create an evolving mural, one that they could look at and add to as they liked. The plan was for the students to collaborate on the mural whenever they had time between class and work or even while they were socializing in the hallway. Mrs. Mochak placed a large roll of paper along one wall in the hallway and invited the students to begin adding drawings and captions, creating a mural that depicted their community. Some included buildings or people they were familiar with, writing underneath the location of the place or who the person was. The students were imagining the real world—their community—and talking, drawing, and writing about it, a very different process than learning from a textbook. With an evolving mural, struggling L2 learners begin to make connections between their world outside and the classroom, all the while linking oral transmission and the written word.

Language Supports

MALP-trained instructors look for opportunities to create materials that will prompt increased student participation and language development. With MALP, the scaffolding can be created spontaneously as needed and serves to demonstrate how the instructor is responsive to the immediate needs of the class.

Word Wall

One widely used language support is a word wall, which in a MALP classroom can take many forms. A word wall must be carefully planned so that it is not just a random list of vocabulary used in class, an alphabetical list, or a list of words supplied by the teacher. Word walls should be organized meaningfully—by content area categories, word families, synonyms, or connectors. In the MALP classroom, the word wall is collaborative, theme-based, and an integral part of the classroom activities. It is organic and evolving. In Mrs. Mochak's literacy class, the students had created a word splash for the word *care*. A word splash, origi-nally developed by Dorsey Hammond of Oakland University in Rochester,

Michigan, and later adapted by many others, is a collection of key terms or concepts of the material students are learning that is "splashed" at odd angles on a chart, blackboard, or other written format (cited in Lipton & Hubble, 2009, p. 82). Mrs. Mochak's word splash for *care* included sentences using *care* as a noun and as a verb, as well as *care* in compound words, such as *daycare*, and care with affixes, such as *careful*.

Sentence Frames

Sentence strips with sentence frames, which provide key words and/or sentence starters, are another common type of language support (Wood, 2002). Sentence frames are consistent with the MALP concept of balancing schemata for struggling L2 learners.

In Mrs. Suoto's class, the students were learning how to define geometric shapes. After the MALP intervention, to guide their language production and to practice the format for defining in an academic setting, she provided:

A _____ (name of shape) is a shape with _____

that has _____.

A right triangle is a shape with three sides that has a 90° angle.

As discussed in Chapter 4, defining is itself a new academic task, which Mrs. Suoto is scaffolding for students. Providing such frames supports academic tasks and literacy, as well as the development of academic language.

Mrs. Suoto had also worked with the students on statements of comparison and contrast. First they created T-charts with lists of items that contrast with each other. She then asked the students to share their statements with one another, and again provided sentence frames:

The _____ differs from the _____.

It differs because the _____ has _____

but the _____ has _____.

The papaya differs from the mango.

It differs because the papaya has many seeds but the mango has a large pit.

Such sentence frames focus the students' attention on the content while reinforcing the particular academic vocabulary and language structures used in presenting the contrast between two items. The balancing of schemata is obvious: The items they are contrasting are familiar while the language and formal schemata are unfamiliar.

Mrs. Mochak was teaching question formation, which is not easy (often students lack sufficient opportunity to practice asking questions in real time) (DeCapua, 2008). As shown in Chapter 6, the instructor asks most of the questions in a classroom, but it is the students who need the practice. It is essential that teachers carefully scaffold question formation by creating sentence frames and posting them as resources so that students have support with the structure of different types of questions. Important vocabulary can also be provided to help in the forming of their questions. As students in Mrs. Mochak's class were about to ask a question, they were able to refer to the frames she provided, which gave them the confidence to ask more questions. Because she found that certain questions frequently arose about procedures and language use, she creates a poster with these sentence frames:

How do you spell _____?

What does _____ mean?

Where is _____?

When is the assignment due?

An alternative is for the teacher to set up a virtual classroom space on the internet where these types of materials can be saved. Today many schools and programs have designated online spaces for teachers and students to post material. The class site can also hold reference materials, activities, and other information as a dynamic ongoing virtual setting.

Equipment and Resources

Classrooms generally contain a variety of equipment and resources to support learning. A MALP classroom is no exception. Here we highlight two areas, electronic equipment and a resource center, and discuss their use in supporting struggling L2 learners.

Using Electronic Equipment

Many schools and programs have limited resources and may not have access to electronic equipment, but we strongly recommend a computer with or without internet access and a document camera. It is extremely helpful to have at least one computer in the MALP classroom so that students can create projects using computer applications; it is also helpful for L2 learners who struggle with writing because keyboarding is often easier than writing by hand (DeCapua, Smathers, & Tang, 2009; DeCapua & Marshall, 2011). Moreover, since one important way learners succeed is by developing the ability to search and find materials, computers with internet access will make this option possible.

The document camera is a rather simple, yet very useful tool. This type of camera is akin to opaque and overhead projectors and is an excellent way to share the work of individual students or groups spontaneously. Mrs. Suoto placed a page from the textbook on the camera so she could clarify an issue for the class; this allowed her to point at something specific to better show the direct connection between her oral explanation and the text. The document camera is particularly well suited to the needs of these students and is consistent with the implementation of MALP.

A Resource Center

A class resource center includes commercially available materials and student-made materials collected over various semesters or even years. Such a class resource center validates students' efforts when they see their work alongside "real" books. Ms. Stein's class produced a welcome booklet, which she used for new incoming students throughout the year. Not only did this booklet provide new students with useful information, but it gave the students who had been involved in its production a strong sense of accomplishment. Because of the booklet's popularity, she continued to use it in subsequent years, with her current students revising portions as necessary (Marshall & DeCapua, 2009).

When struggling L2 learners have access to interesting, culturally relevant print materials, their desire to engage with and understand the material may result in their success with readings beyond their formally assessed level (Bigelow, 2010). As the students develop an affinity for reading, they advance to using print to acquire new information and move further along the right side of the Ways of Learning Continuum. A resource center can offer students a wide variety of sources that will interest them, encouraging students to read texts for required assignments and material they choose voluntarily, both of which are important in promoting literacy skills (Krashen, 2004, 2011).

The resource center is meant to be organic; as the class and teacher produce and discover new material, copies are made available in the resource center, in print and/or digitally. In addition, the resource center has materials available in both English and the native language(s) of the students. Ideally, the resource center will have a computer, e-reader, tablet, digital recorder with headset/ear-buds, and other electronic devices for recording, storing, and playing digital media.

Physical Arrangement

The final component of the MALP classroom is the physical layout, which relates to furniture arrangement and seating. This layout is an important and, at times, neglected aspect, as it can have a significant influence on classroom behaviors. As others have shown (Roskos & Neumann, 2011; Stewart, Evans, & Kaczynski, 1997), the furniture, seating arrangements, and traffic patterns are among key factors that need to be addressed because of how they inform and manage teacher-student and student-student interactions.

To best promote interconnectedness and shared responsibility, the seats and desks or tables in the room need to be moveable if at all possible. The teacher needs to create the expectation that students will be reconfiguring the room based on their needs during particular activities. Ideally, the furniture will allow for different configurations for whole class, group, pair, and individual work. Also, there should be some clear space in front of at least one wall, so that students can approach it to view and discuss the work they have placed there, like murals or posters. If possible, the resource center should have a designated spot in the room.

Sharing a Classroom

Whenever we describe the robust physical setting essential to the implementation of MALP, teachers often raise the issue of the shared classroom. The reality is that many teachers do not have exclusive use of a classroom. A variety of solutions can alleviate this problem. First, a designated corner of the room can usually be set aside for the class and materials left up on the walls and/or rotated for best use of space as needed. Materials can be photographed and saved electronically to be shared, printed, or shown via projection. Also, collaboration among teachers can sometimes result in materials being shared by more than one class using the same room, which adds to the possibilities for establishing a vibrant classroom setting.

Comparing the MALP Physical Environment

In a MALP classroom, all the components work together to create a positive learning climate. A positive classroom climate promotes learning, not just for struggling L2 learners but for all students (Carlson et al, 2006; Dörnyei & Murphy, 2003; Powell, 2011). But what types of things create a more positive classroom and, hence, a positive learning environment? Creating a MALP classroom means creating a community where struggling L2 learners can feel both comfortable and successful as they learn. The three major features of a MALP classroom explored here were the room, especially the walls; the equipment and resources available for learners; and the furniture and physical arrangement. These features are illustrated in Figure 7.1, which summarizes the differences between a MALP classroom and a more traditional teacher-fronted, board-oriented classroom. As this chapter has demonstrated, the physical setting serves to support the implementation of MALP.

The importance of having a space that can be transformed into a home for a learning community cannot be overstated. When students feel comfortable in their physical setting, they are more likely to be attentive, motivated to learn, and contribute to the learning process of others (Dörnyei & Murphy, 2003; Powell, 2011). The room itself becomes a partner in their learning. One MALP-trained teacher tells her students to "read the room," reminding them that the space is filled with resources, ideas, language, and connections to their fellow students. With this discussion of the MALP learning environment, we conclude the presentation of the instructional model and move, in the next and final chapter, to assessing its implementation.

FIGURE 7.1 Comparing the Physical Classroom Environment

Physical Feature	MALP Classroom	Standard Secondary/Adult Education Classroom
Walls	Student work prominently displayed Wide variety of relevant teacher-developed materials evident and accessible, like concept posters Classroom calendar prominently displayed with all personal, school, class events, deadlines Linguistic supports (sentence frames and contextualized word wall items) prominent in room and related to lesson content	Walls contain commercial posters Little or no student work displayed Teacher-developed materials, (concept posters) not evident and/or inaccessible Commercial calendar, if any, with only school items noted Linguistic supports (sentence frames and contextualized word wall items) absent from room and/or are not related to lesson content
Resource Center	Wide variety of student-produced materials evident and accessible Materials in L1 of students displayed and made available Multimedia resources for audio/video as well as print access, in L1 and L2 Age-appropriate, leveled fiction & non-fiction materials available independent reading Internet-based materials/links selected through bookmarking site or other web tool	Few or no student-produced materials Materials provided primarily in L2 Materials include primarily print with very little audio material Internet sites provided with no selection or adaptation for learners
Furniture	Chairs/desks allow for and are consistently used in different configurations for whole class group/pair/individual work If furniture not conducive to different figurations, frequent adaptations can be made for whole class group/pair/individual work	No or minimal flexibility/change in groupings Furniture not conducive to different figurations, and no adjustments made for whole class group/pair/individual work

8

Assessing the
Implementation of MALP

Research on student outcomes assessment tells us that teaching practices greatly influence learner outcomes (Hollins, 2011). The most significant factor affecting student achievement is teacher quality. Teachers make the difference (Harding & Parsons, 2011). As shown throughout this book, the cultural backgrounds of teachers and students, assumptions about ways of learning, and respective priorities all impact the design of instructional experiences and the classroom climate. Effective MALP teachers recognize this and strive to transition struggling L2 learners from the left side of the Ways of Learning Continuum closer to the right end. They understand that implementing all the elements of MALP allows for integration of their disciplinary knowledge with practices that are designed to include the three components of the model: accept learner conditions, combine processes for learning, and focus on new activities with familiar language and content.

Ongoing high-quality assessment and evaluation of the implementation of the MALP model is necessary to ensure that all the elements of MALP are included. Chapter 7 presented a chart showing the elements that should be present in the classroom. This chapter examines project design and lesson delivery, following up on what was discussed in Chapters 5 and 6. The MALP Implementation Rubric is presented in the Appendix to guide educators.

Rubrics are a type of performance assessment with clear, descriptive expectations or criteria to help users focus on what is valued or important (Airiasian & Russell, 2008). They have become a common means for identifying and documenting performance (Usnick & Usnick, 2009). The MALP Rubric is intended to be informational and formative, to be used periodically to assess how well the model is being applied in a given teaching situation. The rubric underscores the essentials of the MALP instructional model, *all* of which must be implemented together, to guard against a piecemeal or partial approach. This assessment tool is an integral part of the MALP model because it assists instructors, supervisors, and trainers in engaging in constructive reflection and dialogue. After reviewing the rubric, instructors can use it to adjust their teaching and classroom. When correctly used, the rubric will help identify missing components and can be the basis for discovering what is missing. Consistent use of the rubric helps implementers of the model to see both their strengths and the areas they need to work on and to track their growth.

Rubric Design

The rubric criteria relate explicitly to the MALP checklist. It has three sections, consistent with the three components and six elements of MALP, and four columns in each section, as shown in Figure 8.1.

    The far left column lists the elements from the MALP Checklist appropriate to each section and component of MALP. On the far left, we see the two elements related to this component, *immediate relevance* and *interconnectedness*.

    The other three columns specify the parameters for MALP pedagogical practices, juxtaposing informal ways of learning on the left and Western-style

FIGURE 8.1 Conditions for Learning

A. Conditions for Learning			
MALP Checklist Element	**Struggling L2 Learner Paradigm**	**Balance of Learner Paradigm and Western-Style Education—MALP**	**Western-Style Formal Education**
Immediate Relevance	All material drawn from students' personal lives	Material drawn from students' personal lives applied to subject areas Connections made to curriculum content	Exclusive focus on subject matter
Interconnectedness	Time devoted to building relationships at expense of focus on course material	Multiple opportunities for students to share personal information and preferences Web of social relationships supports creation of learning community	Total class time devoted to course material at expense of building relationships

formal education on the right; MALP is in the center. We have created the rubric in this way because MALP is a transitional approach between these divergent views of learning originally contrasted in our discussion of the Ways of Learning Continuum. There is one additional element, the balancing of schemata, included in Component C: Activities for Learning.

When working with this rubric, users are asked to evaluate whether observed pedagogical practices for each element of MALP are closer to informal ways of learning in the left-hand column; closer to formal ways of learning in the right-hand column; or if they meet the criteria for MALP-style learning in the center.

Using the MALP Implementation Rubric

To demonstrate use of the MALP Rubric, we visit Mrs. Kassowen who is teaching reading skills to her low-intermediate students.

> Mrs. Kassowen was working with her students on basic reading skills. She had found folktales from different cultures in easy English readers and chose one to begin her unit. After she had begun reading the story, she stopped to ask the students, "What do you think will happen next?" Anaya became extremely upset when Mrs. Kassowen interrupted her reading of the story. Despite her low English proficiency, Anaya was able to convey her dismay at what she viewed as an inappropriate interruption. From her perspective, a story was meant to be told and enjoyed, not used as a tool. (Adapted from Bigelow, 2010)

Mrs. Kassowen felt that her students needed to work on their reading and what better way than to use folktales, something familiar and of high interest across cultures? Mrs. Kassowen tried to engage her students in a series of analytical tasks designed to process the story. Her asking the students to make a prediction is considered a best practice questioning strategy that encourages critical thinking since readers must make logical connections between the text and their ideas to make an informed guess. What Mrs. Kassowen was not aware of was that the act of storytelling is, in Anaya's culture, as important as the story itself. By interrupting the flow as she did, she devalued the experience from Anaya's perspective.

This contrast in priorities can be a major problem for students when encountering oral interaction and oral decontextualized tasks in school settings.

In some cases what teachers have been told are best practices may be counter-productive for struggling L2 students. Listening to their teacher reading aloud is a good example. For these students, the priority is to use their familiar process of oral transmission to experience the reading and become involved in the narrative in the case of a story. At this point while the students see reading as a school activity, they still expect to enjoy a story rather than to analyze it. In formal education, on the other hand, it is a priority to practice and apply academic ways of thinking. For the teacher, simply going through an oral reading of the story would not be considered an effective lesson because the class would not engage in tasks or activities leading to enhanced literacy skills.

What Were the Conditions for Learning?

Immediate Relevance

Mrs. Kassowen does not use any material from the students' lives, although she attempts to make the folktale relevant by asking them to connect the story to events in their own lives. This strategy does not work well because they resist leaving the story to stop and think about themselves. Also, Mrs. Kassowen does not connect with other courses the students may be taking. Therefore, this lessons fails to establish the criterion of immediate relevance. To increase her effectiveness, she could ask the students to bring a story with them or to tell her about a story that she can research and bring in to class to share.

Interconnectedness

Mrs. Kassowen creates a warm, supportive setting by having the students gather around her and by asking them to listen to each other's comments about the story. However, the focus is on the information and not on relationships and interactions among the members of the class. Her classroom dynamic follows the IRE or IRF patterns (see Chapter 6), with communication occurring only between teacher and student and not among the students. To expand the classroom use of relationships, she and the students can create their own folktale as a project, increasing both relevance and interconnectedness as they relate the story to experiences in their own lives.

Regarding accepting conditions for learning, Mrs. Kassowen has made efforts to establish these, but still needs to move closer to MALP. Referring to Figure 8.1, readers will see that her lesson primarily includes items from the right-hand column, Western-style formal education.

What Were the Processes for Learning?

The context for learning must be a positive and supportive learning environment where the students, teacher, and learning materials mesh synergistically. Both collaborative work and individual work are integrated into this learning context. Teachers guide students in their learning process while carefully monitoring that they have multiple opportunities for individual and shared learning.

There are subtle but important differences in how teachers approach group and individual contributions to learning. In the informal setting, learners are accustomed to individuals who are more expert being the resources for other learners who cannot perform a given task on their own. The strong learners will always be available for assistance, so there is no need within the group for the weaker ones to become skilled at a particular task.

In the formal setting, each learner feels personally responsible for the task required and even if the group is working together, students will perform on their own in due time. There is no expectation for the more adept learners to assist others in the group with their work although it may be encouraged. In fact, it is common to hear students say, "I did my share."

MALP combines these perspectives—members of a group are expected to help each other, not only for the specific tasks at hand, but also toward the goal of each group member rising to the level of performing the task independently. Individual accomplishment is important, but equally important is the expectation that each individual will help if needed, as exemplified in the aphorism, "A rising tide lifts all boats." See Figure 8.2 for a closer look at using this part of the rubric.

Group Responsibility Leading to Individual Accountability

Mrs. Kassowen is engaging in direct instruction with each student accountable for learning. Interaction and sharing is minimal as she focuses on individual responses (see the discussion of IRE and IRF in Chapter 6). Because the students are not in pairs or small groups but acting as a class group, they do not have the opportunity to read and listen to each other, to stop and discuss the story if they have questions, or to connect their own experience with the folktale.

Oral Transmission to Scaffold the Written Word

Mrs. Kassowen does an excellent job of linking the oral and written by asking the students to follow along with her as she reads the story. She checks to make sure that everyone is on the same page, and she uses her finger to show where

FIGURE 8.2 Processes for Learning

B. Processes for Learning			
MALP Checklist Element	Struggling L2 Learner Paradigm	Balance of Learner Paradigm and Western-Style Education—MALP	Western-Style Formal Education
Group Responsibility Leading to Individual Accountability	Focus of group is cohesion rather than uplifting individuals to new learning levels, so weaker students continue to rely on stronger ones	Full evidence of both joint and individual contributions embedded in each activity Peer instruction the norm	Instruction focused on individual contributions
Oral Transmission to Scaffold Written Word	Oral transmission processes used exclusively Separation of oral/written modes in class activities	Teacher consistently combines oral transmission with written word	Focus on written word for obtaining meaning and learning new material Print not scaffolded through oral interaction

she is. Her use of the document camera facilities this. She pauses to check in with students and so she can ask them about the language of the story. Since Mrs. Kassowen does not present the story via media, however, the students cannot pause, rewind, and listen again.

With respect to the combination of processes for learning, Mrs. Kassowen makes a good effort at using the oral to scaffold the written text, but to work within MALP, she needs to be more focused on the processes, not just the analysis of the text. In terms of gradually leading the students toward individual accountability, she needs to restructure her tasks to provide ways for the students to use each other as they learn.

Mrs. Kassowen could flip her classroom, which would enable her to record the folktale but also show her finger moving with the words. Then in class, the students could work together to do tasks she assigns.

Component C: Activities for Learning

Teachers are responsible for designing learning tasks appropriate for their students, which should be sequentially progressive, developmentally appropriate, and maximally engaging to foster successful and productive learning (Ball & Forzini, 2009). The challenges when working with struggling adolescent and adult L2 learners are both recognizing where the baseline is for this progression and understanding what developmentally appropriate and maximally engaging tasks are. The learning tasks must be presented so that students increase their understanding of key concepts and are able to make connections between prior knowledge and the new information (Sousa, 2012). In other words, these tasks must be *comprehensible*. And in the MALP instructional model, task comprehension is based on schema.

Tasks Requiring Academic Ways of Thinking

Mrs. Kassowen clearly selected the concept of prediction as the focus of her lesson. When she teaches them to stop and to think about what might happen next as they go through the story, it builds a new schema for them. Although predicting may seem contextualized in this case because the narrative provides the context, the fact that they are being asked to interrupt the flow of the narrative means that they must remove themselves as listeners and instead provide metacognitive insights. Thus, they are performing a decontextualized task.

Decontextualized Tasks Accessible Through Familiar Language and Content

Mrs. Kassowen believes she is making the prediction task accessible through use of a folktale, rather than using subject matter from the curriculum. She hopes that the language and content of the story will be familiar enough to the students without being 100 percent familiar so that she can help them attend more closely to the task of making predictions as they read.

Regarding the activities for learning, Mrs. Kassowen has created a pathway for her students to master a new schema of predicting and successfully uses MALP in this way. She demonstrates how a teacher can balance the schemata to introduce a new way of thinking. See Figure 8.3 to see how the activities for learning are involved.

Balancing of Schemata

Readers will notice that Figure 8.3 includes an element that does not appear on the MALP Checklist (see Chapter 3). This additional element calls for a balancing of the three schemata. While MALP focuses primarily on building new formal schemata through accessible language and content, it is equally essential that teachers help struggling L2 learners build new linguistic and content schemata, as presented and discussed in Chapter 4. This element of the rubric is designed to ensure that the teacher is attending to all three schemata and balancing them appropriately for the students. With MALP, the three schemata are balanced when the focus is on *one* of the three so that the third one, the new schema, is solidly scaffolded to help that students gain mastery in all areas. In other words, if the *language* is new, the teacher scaffolds it by relying on familiar tasks and content. If *content* is new, the teacher introduces it using familiar tasks and language.

Chapter 6 presented an example of how Mrs. Schwartz successfully balanced the schemata using the flipped classroom model to teach Boyle's Law. She used oral transmission (video lectures) and demonstrations to convey language and content. After laying the foundation, she introduced the language necessary for explaining the concept of inverse proportion. Finally, she presented the scientific and mathematical content of Boyle's Law, drawing from physics and chemistry.

Unlike Mrs. Schwartz, the teachers described in Chapter 3, Mr. Morris and Mrs. Shim, did not successfully balance the three schemata. In Mr. Morris's lessons on families, all three schemata were familiar, hindering opportunities for building new schemata. He used only familiar tasks, the native language or already mastered aspects of the new language, and content from native culture or already familiar L2 culture. The family collage project, while engaging for the students and excellent for increasing interconnectedness and shared responsibility, did not include the types of decontextualized tasks necessary for their transition to success in school settings.

In the case of Mrs. Shim and the microscope lesson, the opposite is true. All three schemata were unfamiliar, making the lesson inaccessible to students. Mrs. Shim used vocabulary and structures well beyond the students' proficiency level to present new subject area content and did so through largely unfamiliar decontextualized tasks, such as defining, categorizing, and analyzing. Her lesson on the use of the microscope was not effective because learners found this lesson challenging, perplexing, and frustrating. The lesson, while a valuable one, failed to facilitate student learning and was not effective.

FIGURE 8.3 Activities for Learning

C. Activities for Learning			
MALP Checklist Element	Struggling L2 Learner Paradigm	Balance of Learner Paradigm and Western-Style Education—MALP	Western-Style Formal Education
Tasks Requiring Academic Ways of Thinking	Decontextualized tasks not evident in instruction	Decontextualized task objective included Decontextualized task targets specific academic ways of thinking	Decontextualized tasks included and expected but not as learning objectives
Decontextualized Tasks Accessible through Familiar Language and Content	No scaffolding of tasks attempted as tasks are already familiar	New decontextualized task (formal schema) introduced and scaffolded via familiar language and content	New decontextualized task presented along with new academic content and language
Balancing of Schemata[1]	Schemata unbalanced: all familiar Only familiar language, content, and formal schemata included Opportunities for building new schemata lacking	Schemata balanced: MALP New task scaffolded by familiar language and content New language scaffolded by familiar task and content New content scaffolded by familiar language and task	Schemata unbalanced: all unfamiliar Only familiar language, content, and schemata included Opportunities for using familiar schemata to access new schemata lacking

[1] Additional element not on original MALP Checklist.

Let's return to Mrs. Kassowen's instruction on predictions. Once the concept of prediction is introduced to students, she can reinforce this formal schema and focus on the other two. How might she do this? Mrs. Kassowen could let the other teachers know that she has worked on prediction and ask them to give students the opportunity to use this new knowledge in their other classes. She might decide to ask the students to share how they have used predictions in other situations, both in and out of school.

To introduce prediction, Mrs. Kassowen could practice expressions commonly used to make predictions, such as *it is likely/possible/probable that…* or through modals, like *might, may*, or *could*. She could also introduce phrases to provide support for a prediction, such as *based on* or *given that.* If she follows MALP, this language would be accompanied by content that is familiar, immediately relevant, and shared. To scaffold new content, Mrs. Kassowen could then draw from what the students are learning about in other classes or could incorporate new content into a MALP project (DeCapua & Marshall, 2010a, 2011).

This analysis of Mrs. Kassowen's lesson provides one example of how the MALP Implementation Rubric can be used as a teacher evaluation tool. Mrs. Kassowen does well on the activities for learning, including the balancing of schemata. She has made a good effort in terms of immediate relevance and on scaffolding the written word, but could move more toward the MALP model. She should work more on interconnectedness and shared responsibility. Many teachers will, like Mrs. Kassowen, have a mix of teaching practices, that, in some cases, bring them closer to and in others farther away from the MALP model. The rubric is designed to help teachers to come to the middle, a mutually adaptive place in their teaching. As teachers strive to incorporate MALP in their classrooms, they can benefit from a self-assessment of their instruction.

Culturally Responsive Teaching: MALP

Chapter 2 focused on culture, communication, and learning with the ICF. This framework can now be recast in light of the MALP Implementation Rubric and Culturally Responsive Teaching (Ladson-Billings, 1994; Gay, 2000). We now look at Mr. Morris and Mrs. Shim and how they demonstrated that their teaching is culturally responsible as they follow the principles of the ICF.

Teachers like Mr. Morris who are clearly trying to match their teaching to the backgrounds and needs of the learners do an excellent job of the first guideline for the framework: establishing and maintaining an ongoing, two-way relationship. However, in his desire to be culturally responsive, Mr. Morris neglects the key priorities of the Western-style paradigm that will ensure his students' success. He also fails to build associations between the familiar and unfamiliar schemata. As the rubric shows, his teaching remains, for all three components of MALP, in the left-hand column. Although his teaching might be characterized as culturally responsive, truly responsive teaching assists learners with the types of tasks and skills required by the system in which they are being educated. Here Mr. Morris falls short of the mark.

Teachers like Mrs. Shim, fare even worse when viewed through the dual lenses of the ICF and culturally responsive teaching. Mrs. Shim faithfully implements the Western-style learning paradigm and makes little or no attempt to develop two-way relationships, honor learner priorities, or make associations with familiar schemata for her learners. Her teaching is not designed to be culturally responsive. She teaches her struggling L2 learners as if they were native speakers of the language, members of the mainstream culture, and familiar with academic ways of thinking in formal education. In short, she teaches these students the same way that she teaches all students. Her teaching, according to the rubric, rests squarely in the right hand column. She makes no cultural accommodations or adaptations.

We believe that culturally responsive teaching can bridge the divide between the students and their potential achievement. Such teaching does not look like Mrs. Shim's approach, nor does it look like that of Mr. Morris. In the MALP model, the priorities of both paradigms are incorporated. Being truly culturally responsive means being responsive to both the needs of the learner and the need to educate them within the context of scholastic culture (Nieto, 2010). Barring any major paradigm shifts in the Western-style educational model, instruction that does not include scholastic culture in its design will shortchange struggling L2 learners.

To effectively meet the needs of such learners, teachers must strike a balance, as shown in the implementation of MALP, a transitional approach between the two paradigms. MALP is best exemplified by Mrs. Schwartz whose flipped classroom and lesson on Boyle's Law in Chapter 6 illustrated the middle column of the rubric. This model represents culturally responsive teaching in the best sense because it takes elements of each culturally based learning paradigm to forge one based on mutual adaptation. Teachers who are guided by MALP and use the MALP Implementation Rubric will find that their struggling L2 learners will respond to instruction, take ownership of their learning, and make significant strides towards achieving their educational goals.

Appendix

MALP Implementation Rubric

A. Conditions for Learning			
MALP Checklist Element	**Struggling L2 Learner Paradigm**	**Balance of Learner Paradigm and Western-Style Education—MALP**	**Western-Style Formal Education**
Immediate Relevance	All material drawn from students' personal lives	Material drawn from students' personal lives applied to subject areas Connections made to curriculum content	Exclusive focus on subject matter
Interconnectedness	Time devoted to building relationships at expense of focus on course material	Multiple opportunities for students to share personal information and preferences Web of social relationships supports creation of learning community	Total class time devoted to course material at expense of building relationships

B. Processes for Learning			
MALP Checklist Element	**Struggling L2 Learner Paradigm**	**Balance of Learner Paradigm and Western-Style Education—MALP**	**Western-Style Formal Education**
Group Responsibility Leading to Individual Accountability	Focus of group is cohesion rather than uplifting individuals to new learning levels, so weaker students continue to rely on stronger ones	Full evidence of both joint and individual contributions embedded in each activity Peer instruction the norm	Instruction focused on individual contributions
Oral Transmission to Scaffold Written Word	Oral transmission processes used exclusively Separation of oral/written modes in class activities	Teacher consistently combines oral transmission with written word	Focus on written word for obtaining meaning and learning new material Print not scaffolded through oral interaction

C. Activities for Learning			
MALP Checklist Element	**Struggling L2 Learner Paradigm**	**Balance of Learner Paradigm and Western-Style Education—MALP**	**Western-Style Formal Education**
Tasks Requiring Academic Ways of Thinking	Decontextual-ized tasks not evident in instruction	Decontextualized task objective included Decontextualized task targets specific academic ways of thinking	Decontextual-ized tasks included and expected but not as learning objectives
Decontextualized Tasks Accessible through Familiar Language and Content	No scaffolding of tasks attempted as tasks are already familiar	New decontextualized task (formal schema) introduced and scaffolded via familiar language and content	New decontex-tualized task presented along with new academic content and language
Balancing of Schemata[1]	Schemata unbalanced: all familiar Only familiar language, content, and formal schemata included Opportunities for building new schemata lacking	Schemata balanced: MALP New task scaffolded by famiiar language and content New language scaffolded by familiar task and content New content scaffolded by familiar language and task	Schemata unbalanced: all unfamiliar Only familiar language, content, and schemata included Opportunities for using familiar schemata to access new schemata lacking

[1] Additional element not on original MALP Checklist.

References

Abd-Kadir, J., & Hardman, F. (2007). The discourse of whole class teaching: A comparative study of Kenyan and Nigerian primary English lessons. *Language and Education, 21,* 1–15.

Airasian, P., & Russell, M. (2008). *Classroom assessment: Concepts and applications* (6th ed.). New York: McGraw-Hill.

Al-Amoush, S.A., Markic, S., Abu-Hola, I., & Eilks, I. (2011). Jordanian prospective and experienced chemistry teachers' beliefs about teaching and learning and their potential for educational reform. *Science Education International, 22,* 185–201.

Anderson, L. W., & Krathwohl, D. R. (Eds.). (2001). *A taxonomy for learning, teaching and assessing: A revision of Bloom's Taxonomy of educational objectives.* New York: Longman.

Anderson-Levitt, K. (2003). *Local meanings, global schooling.* Hampshire, U.K.: Palgrave.

Andrews, J., & Yee, W.C. (2006). Children's "Funds of Knowledge" and their real life activities: Two minority ethnic children learning in out-of-school contexts in the UK. *Educational Review, 58,* 435–449.

Armstrong, T. (2009). *Multiple intelligences in the classroom* (3rd ed.). Alexandria, VA: Association for Supervision and Curriculum Development.

Asher, J. (1969). The total physical response approach to second language learning. *The Modern Language Journal, 53,* 3–17.

Auerbach, E. (1989). Toward a social-contextual approach to family literacy. *Harvard Educational Review, 59,* 165–181.

August, A., Goldenberg, C., & Rueda, R. (2006). Native American children and youth: Culture, language, and literacy. *Journal of American Indian Education, 35,* 24–37.

Ball, D., & Forzani, F. (2009). The work of teaching and the challenge for teacher education. *Journal of Teacher Education, 60,* 497–511.

Battiste, M., & Henderson, J.Y. (2000). *Protecting indigenous knowledge and heritage: A global challenge.* Saskatoon, SK: Purich.

Bearne, E. (1999). *Use of language across the secondary curriculum.* London: Routledge.

Bergmann, J., & Sams, A. (2009). Remixing chemistry class: Two Colorado teachers make vodcasts of their lectures to free up class time for hands-on activities. *Learning & Leading with Technology, 36,* 22–27.

Bernardo, A. B. I. (2003). On defining and developing literacy across communities. *International Review of Education, 46,* 455–464.

Bigelow, M. (2010). *Mogadishu on the Mississippi: Language, racialized identity and education in a new land.* Malden, MA: Wiley-Blackwell.

Bloom, B. (1956). *Taxonomy of educational objectives, Handbook I: The cognitive domain.* New York: David McKay.

Blum-Kulka, S., Huck-Taglicht, D., Avni, H. (2004). The social and discursive spectrum of peer talk. *Discourse Studies, 6,* 307–328.

Brown, H. D. (2007). *Principles of language learning and teaching* (5th ed.). White Plains, NY: Pearson.

Bruner, J. (1961). The act of discovery. *Harvard Educational Review, 31,* 21–32.

Bulut, M. (2006). Curriculum reform in Turkey: A case of primary school mathematics curriculum. *Eurasia Journal of Mathematics, Science & Technology Education, 3,* 203–212.

Calkins, L. (1994). *The art of teaching writing.* Portsmouth, NH: Heinemann.

Carlson, R., Dwyer, K., Bingham, S., Cruz, A., Prisbell, M., & Fus, D. (2006). Connected classroom climate and communication apprehension: Correlations and implications for the basic course. *Basic Communication Course Annual, 18,* 1–27.

Carrell, P.L., Devine, J. & Eskey, D. (Eds.). (1988). *Interactive approaches to second language reading.* Cambridge, U.K.: Cambridge University Press.

Cazden, C. (1988). *Classroom discourse: The language of teaching and learning.* Portsmouth, NH: Heinemann.

Cazden, C. (2001). *Classroom discourse: The language of teaching and learning* (2nd ed.). Portsmouth, NH: Heinemann.

Chamot, A., & O'Malley, J. (1994). *The CALLA handbook: Implementing the cognitive academic language learning approach.* White Plains, NY: Addison Wesley Longman.

Cherney, I. (2008). The effects of active learning on students' memories for course content. *Active Learning in Higher Education, 9,* 152–171.

Chitty, C. (2002). *Understanding schools and schooling.* London: Falmer Press.

Chung, T., & Mallery, P. (2000). Social comparison, individualism-collectivism, and self-esteem in China and the United States. *Current Psychology, 18,* 340–352.

Cole, M. (2005). Cross-cultural and historical perspectives on the developmental consequences of education. *Human Development, 48,* 195–216.

Collins, J.L. (1998). *Strategies for struggling writers.* New York: Guilford Press.

Cornwall, A. (1992). *Body mapping in health. RRA Notes, 16,* 69–76. London: International Institute of Environment and Development.

Cottrell, S. (2001). *Teaching study skills and supporting learning.* Basingstoke, U.K.: Palgrave.

Cummins, J. (1982). *Bilingualism and minority language children.* Toronto: OISE Press.

Cummins, J. (2001). *Negotiating identities: Education for empowerment in a diverse society* (2nd ed.). Los Angeles: California Association for Bilingual Education.

Cummins, J., Brown, K., & Sayers, D. (2007). *Literacy, technology, and diversity: Teaching for success in changing times.* Boston: Pearson.

DeCapua, A. (2008). *Grammar for teachers: A guide to American English for native and non-native speakers.* Boston: Springer.

DeCapua, A., & Marshall, H. W. (2010a). Serving ELLs with limited or interrupted education: Intervention that works. *TESOL Journal, 1,* 49–70.

DeCapua A., & Marshall, H. W. (2010b). Students with limited or interrupted formal education in U.S. classrooms. *Urban Review, 42,* 159–173.

DeCapua, A., & Marshall, H. W. (2011). *Breaking new ground: Teaching students with limited or interrupted formal education.* Ann Arbor: University of Michigan Press.

DeCapua, A., Smathers, W., & Tang, F. (2009). *Meeting the needs of students with limited or interrupted schooling: A guide for educators.* Ann Arbor: University of Michigan Press.

DeCapua, A., & Wintergerst, A. (2004). *Crossing cultures in the language classroom*. Ann Arbor: University of Michigan Press.

Deutscher, G. (2010). *Through the looking glass: Why the world looks different in other languages*. New York: Metropolitan.

Dixon, C., & Nessel, D. (1990). *Language experience approach to reading (and writing)*. Englewood Cliffs, NJ: Prentice Hall.

Dörnyei, Z., & Murphy, T. (2003). *Group dynamics in the language classroom*. Cambridge, U.K.: Cambridge University Press.

Dyer, C., & Choksi, A. (2001). Literacy, schooling, & development: Views of Rabaris nomads, India. In B. Street (Ed.), *Literacy and development: Ethnographic perspectives* (pp. 27–39). New York: Routledge.

Echevarria, J., Vogt, M.E., & Short, D. (2008). *Making content comprehensible for English language learners: The SIOP model* (3rd ed.). Boston: Allyn & Bacon.

Eisenstein, E. (1979). *The printing press as an agent of change: Communications and cultural transformations in early-modern Europe*. New York: Cambridge University Press.

Estes, T., Mintz, S., & Gunter, M.A. (2011). *Instructions: A models approach* (6th ed.). Boston: Allyn & Bacon.

Ferris, D., & Hedgcock, J. (2004). *Teaching ESL composition: Purpose, process, and practice* (2nd ed.). Mahwah, NJ: Lawrence Erlbaum.

Flynn, J. (2007). *What is intelligence?* New York: Cambridge University Press.

Frayer, D., Frederick, W. C., & Klausmeier, H. J. (1969). *A schema for testing the level of cognitive mastery*. Madison: Wisconsin Center for Education Research.

Fredricks, J., Blumenfeld, P., & Paris, A. (2004). School engagement: Potential of the concept, state of the evidence. *Review of Educational Research, 74,* 59–109.

Freeman, D., Freeman, Y., & Mercuri, S. (2002). *Closing the achievement gap: How to reach limited-formal-schooling and long-term English learners*. Portsmouth, NH: Heinemann.

Fuligini, A., Tseng, V., & Lam, M. (1999). Attitudes toward family obligations among American adolescents with Asian, Latin American, and European backgrounds. *Child Development, 70,* 1030–1044.

Gahungu, A., Gahungu, O., & Luseno, F. (2011, April 15). Educating culturally displaced students with truncated formal education (CDS-TFE): The case of refugee students and challenges for administrators, teachers, and counselors. Retrieved from http://cnx.org/content/m37446/1.1/

Gass, S., & Selinker, L. (2008). *Second language acquisition: An introductory course* (3rd ed.). New York: Routledge.

Gay, G. (2000). *Culturally responsive teaching: Theory, research, and practice*. New York: Teachers College Press.

Gay, G. (2002). Preparing for culturally responsive teaching. *Journal of Teacher Education, 53,* 106–116.

Gee, J. (2007). *Social linguistics and literacies: Ideology in discourses* (3rd ed.). London: Taylor and Francis.

Genesee, F., Lindholm-Leary, K., Saunders, W., & Christian, D. (2006). *Educating English language learners*. New York: Cambridge University Press.

González, N., Moll, L., and Amanti, C. (2005). *Funds of knowledge: Theorizing practices in households, communities, and classrooms.* Mahwah, NJ: Lawrence Erlbaum.

Greenfield, P., Quiroz, B., & Raeff, C. (2000). Cross-cultural conflict and harmony in the social construction of the child. In S. Harkness, C. Raeff, & C.M. Super (Eds.), *Variability in the social construction of the child* (pp. 93–108). (*New directions in child development*, No. 87.) San Francisco: Jossey-Bass.

Grigorenko, E. (2007). Hitting, missing, and in between: A typology of the impact of western education on the non-western world. *Comparative Education, 43,* 165–186.

Guha, S. (2006). Using mathematics strategies in early childhood education as a basis for culturally responsive teaching. *International Journal of Early Years Education, 14,* 15–34.

Gutiérrez, K. (2008). Developing a sociocritical literacy in the third space. *Reading Research Quarterly, 43,* 148–164.

Gutiérrez, K., Baquedano-Lopez, P., & Tejada, C. (1999). Rethinking diversity: Hybridity and hybrid language practices in the Third Space. *Mind, Culture, and Activity, 6,* 286–303.

Hall, E. T. (1966). *The hidden dimension.* New York: Anchor Books.

Harding, K., & Parsons, J. (2011). Improving teacher education programs. *Australian Journal of Teacher Education, 36,* 51–61.

Hewlitt, P. (2011). Conceptual physics, Chapter 14, Gases [PowerPoint slides] Retrieved from Witt/Lyons/Suchocki/Yeh, Conceptual integrated science faculty.

Hickling-Hudson, A., & Ahlquist, R. (2003). Contesting the curriculum in the schooling of indigenous children in Australia and the United States: From Eurocentrism to culturally powerful pedagogies. *Comparative Education Review, 47,* 64–89.

Hofling, C. (1993). Marking space and time in Itzaj Maya narrative. *Journal of Linguistic Anthropology, 3,* 164–184.

Hofstede, G., & Hofstede, G. J., & Minkov, M. (2010). *Cultures and organizations: Software for the mind* (3rd ed.). New York: McGraw-Hill.

Hofstede, G., & McCrae, R. R. (2004). Personality and culture revisited: Linking traits and dimensions of culture. *Cross-Cultural Research: The Journal of Comparative Social Science, 38,* 52–88.

Hollins, E. (2011). Teacher preparation for quality teaching. *Journal of Teacher Education, 64,* 395–407.

Hsu, F. L. K. (1985). The self in cross-cultural perspective. In A. Marsella, G. de Vos, & F. Hsu (Eds.), *Culture and self: Asian and Western perspectives* (pp. 24–55). New York: Tavistock.

Ibarra, R. (2001). *Beyond affirmative action: Reframing the context of higher education.* Madison: The University of Wisconsin Press.

Illich, I. (1973). *De-schooling society.* New York: Penguin.

Jezewski, M.A., & Sotnik, P. (2001). *The rehabilitation service provider as culture broker: Providing culturally competent services to foreign-born persons.* Buffalo, NY: Center for International Rehabilitation Research Information and Exchange. Retrieved from http://cirrie.buffalo.edu/culture/monographs/cb.php

Jiménez, R., García, G., & Pearson, D. (1996). The reading strategies of bilingual Latina/o students who are successful English readers: Opportunities and obstacles. *Reading Research Quarterly, 31,* 90–112.

Johnson, M. (2000). The view from the *Wuro*: A guide to child rearing for Fulani parents. In J. DeLoache & A. Gottliebe, (Eds.), *A world of babies: Imagined childcare guides for seven societies* (pp. 171–198). New York: Cambridge University Press.

Joyce, B., Weil, M., & Calhoun, E. (2009). *Models of teaching* (8th ed.). Boston: Allyn & Bacon.

Kağitçibaşi, C., Göksen, F., & Gülgöz, S. (2005). Functional adult literacy and empowerment of women: Impact of a functional literacy program in Turkey. *Journal of Adolescent & Adult Literacy, 44*, 458–466.

Kanu, Y. (2007). Increasing school success among aboriginal students: Culturally responsive curriculum or macrostructural variables affecting schooling? *Diaspora, Indigenous, and Minority Education, 1*, 21–41.

Khan, R. (2011). *Meeting the needs of English language learners with interruptions in their formal schooling: A comparative case study of two teachers' classrooms.* Unpublished dissertation. Toronto: University of Toronto Press.

King, A. (Winter, 1993). From sage on the stage to guide on the side. *Teaching, 41*, 30–35.

Kozulin, A., Gindis, B., Ageyev, V. S., & Miller, S. M. (2003). *Vygotsky's educational theory in cultural context.* New York: Cambridge University Press.

Krashen, S. (2004). *The power of reading* (2nd ed.). Portsmouth, NH: Heinemann.

Krashen, S. (2011). Protecting students against the effects of poverty: Libraries. *New England Reading Association Journal, 46*, 17–21.

Kuhn, D. (2009). Do students need to be taught to reason? *Educational Research Review, 4*, 1–6.

Kuhn, T. (1970). *The structure of scientific revolutions* (2nd ed.). Chicago: University of Chicago Press.

Ladson-Billings, G. (1994). *The dreamkeepers: Successful teachers for African-American children.* San Francisco: Jossey-Bass.

Ladson-Billings, G. (1995). Toward a theory of culturally relevant pedagogy. *American Educational Research Journal, 32*(3), 465–491.

Ladson-Billings, G. (2009). *The dreamkeepers* (2nd ed.). San Francisco: Jossey-Bass.

Lage, M., Platt, G., & Treglia, M. (2000). Inverting the classroom: A gateway to creating an inclusive learning environment. *Journal of Economic Education, 31*, 30–43.

Lakoff, G. (1990). *Women, fire, and dangerous things.* Chicago: Chicago University Press.

Lemann, N. (2000). *The big test.* New York: Farrar, Strauss, and Giroux.

Leung, F. (2001). In search of an East Asian identity in mathematics education. *Educational Studies in Mathematics, 47*, 35–51.

Liang, X. (2004). Cooperative learning as a sociocultural practice. *The Canadian Modern Language Review, 60*, 637–668.

Lipton, L., & Hubble, D. (2009). *More than 50 ways to learner-centered literacy* (2nd ed.). Thousand Oaks, CA: Corwin.

Lu, H.L., & Bodur, Y. (2011). A literature review of East Asian Americans' cultures and behaviors: Meeting students' cultural needs in schools. *International Journal of Humanities and Social Science, 1*, 59–69.

Luk, J. C. M., & Lin, A. M. Y. (2007). *Classroom interactions as cross-cultural encounters: Native speakers in EFL lessons.* Mahwah, NJ: Lawrence Erlbaum.

Lynch, J. (2009). Print literacy engagement of parents from low-income backgrounds: Implications for adult and family literacy programs. *Journal of Adolescent & Adult Literacy, 52,* 509–521.

MacDonald, J. W. (1988). Theory-practice and the hermeneutic circle. In W. Pinar (Ed.), *Contemporary curriculum discourses* (pp. 86–116). Scottsdale, AZ: Gorsuch Scarisbrick.

Marshall, H. W. (1994). Hmong/English bilingual adult literacy project. Final report of research conducted under the National Institute for Literacy, grant #X257A20457. University of Wisconsin–Green Bay.

Marshall, H. W. (1998). A mutually adaptive learning paradigm (MALP) for Hmong students. *Cultural Circles, 3,* 134–141.

Marshall, H. W., & DeCapua, A. (2009). Glue: A technique for eliminating fragments and run-ons. *The CATESOL Journal, 21,* 175–184.

Marshall, H. W., & DeCapua A. (2010). The newcomer booklet: A project for limited formally schooled students. *ELT Journal, 64,* 396–404.

Marshall, H. W., & DeCapua, A., & Antolini, C. (2010). Engaging English language learners with limited or interrupted formal education. *Educator's Voice, 3,* 56–65.

Martin, J. R., & Rose, D. (2003). *Working with discourse: Meaning beyond the clause.* London: Continuum.

Martínez, I. (2009). What's age gotta do with it? Understanding the age-identities and school-going practices of Mexican immigrant youth in New York City. *High School Journal, 92,* 34–48.

Mazur, E. (1997). *Peer instruction: A user's manual.* White Plains, NY: Pearson Benjamin Cummings.

McBrien, J. L. (2011). The importance of context: Vietnamese, Somali, and Iranian refugee mothers discuss their resettled lives and involvement in their children's schools. *A Journal of Comparative and International Education, 41,* 75–90.

McCarthy, M., & O'Keeffe, A. (2004). Research on the teaching of speaking. *Annual Review of Applied Linguistics, 24,* 26–43.

McVee, M. B., Dunsmore, K., & Gavelek, J. R. (2005). Schema theory revisited. *Review of Educational Research, 75,* 531–566.

Mehan, H. (1979) *Learning lessons: Social organization in the classroom.* Cambridge, MA: Harvard University Press.

Menken, K. (2008). *English learners left behind: Standardized testing as language policy.* Clevedon, U.K.: Multilingual Matters.

Mohr, K. J., & Mohr, E. S. (2007, February). Extending English-language learners' classroom interactions using the response protocol. *The Reading Teacher, 60,* 440–450.

Mrowicki, L. (1990). *First words in English: Book 1.* Palatine, IL: Linmore Publishing.

Musumeci, D. (1996). Teacher–learner negotiation in content-based instruction: Communication at cross-purposes? *Applied Linguistics, 17,* 286–325.

National Research Council (2007). *Taking science to school.* Washington, DC: National Academies Press.

Nieto, S. (2010). *Language, culture, and teaching: Critical perspectives* (2nd ed.). New York: Routledge.

Nisbett, R. (2003). *The geography of thought: How Asians and Westerners think differently and why.* New York: Free Press.

Noor, R. (2001). Contrastive rhetoric in expository prose: Approaches and achievements. *Journal of Pragmatics, 33,* 255–269.

Nystrand, M., Wu, L., Gamoran, A., Zeiser, S., & Long, D. (2003, March-April). Questions in time: Investigating the structure and dynamics of unfolding classroom discourse. *Discourse Processes, 35,* 135–196.

Ochs, E., & Schiefflin, B. (1985). Language acquisition and socialization. In R. Shweder & R. LeVine (Eds.), *Culture theory: Essays on mind, self, and emotion* (pp. 276–320). New York: Cambridge University Press.

Offit, T. (2008). *Conquistadores de la calle: Child street labor in Guatemala City.* Austin: University of Texas Press.

O'Keeffe, A., McCarthy, M., & Carter, R. (2007). *From corpus to classroom: Language use and language teaching.* Cambridge, U.K.: Cambridge University Press.

O'Malley, J. M., & Chamot, A. U. (1990). *Learning strategies in second language acquisition.* Cambridge, U.K.: Cambridge University Press.

Ong, W. (1982). *Orality and literacy: The technologizing of the word.* New York: Methuen.

Oyserman, D., & Lee, S. (2008). Does culture influence what and how we think? Effects of priming, individualism and collectivism. *Psychological Bulletin, 134,* 311–342.

Ozmon, H., & Carver, S. (2008). *Philosophical foundations of education* (8th ed.). Upper Saddle River, NJ: Pearson.

Paradise, R., & Rogoff, B. (2009). Side by side: Learning by observing and pitching in. *Ethos, 37,* 102–138.

Parrish, B., & Johnson, K. (April 2010). Promoting learner transitions to postsecondary education and work: Developing academic readiness skills from the beginning. *CAELA Network Brief.* U.S. Department of Education. Retrieved from www.cal.org/caelanetwork/resources/transitions.html

Peña, E. D., & Mendez-Perez, A. (2006). Individualistic and collectivistic approaches to language learning. *Zero to Three, 27,* 31–41.

Peregoy, S., & Boyle, O. (2008). *Reading, writing, and learning in ESL: A resource book for teaching K–12 learners* (5th ed). New York: Pearson.

Petersson, K., Reis, A., Askelöf, S., Castro-Caldas, A., & Ingvar, M. (2000). Language processing modulated by literacy: A network analysis of verbal repetition in literate and illiterate subjects. *Journal of Cognitive Neuroscience, 12,* 364–382.

Pew Research Hispanic Report. (2013). *Statistical portrait of the foriegn-born population in the United States.* Retrieved from http://pewhispanic.org/2013/01/29/statistical_portrait_of_the_foriegn_born_population_in_the_United_States-2011

Pon, G., Goldstein, T., & Schecter, S. R. (2003). Interrupted by silences: The contemporary education of Hong Kong-born Chinese Canadians. In R. Bayley & S. R. Schecter (Eds.), *Language socialization in bilingual and multilingual societies* (pp. 114–127). Clevedon, U.K.: Multilingual Matters.

Pontefract, C., & Hardman, F. (2005). Classroom discourse in Kenyan primary schools. *Comparative Education, 2,* 87–106.

Powell, R. (2011). Classroom climate/physical environment: Creating an inclusive community. In R. Powell & E.C. Rightmyer (Eds.), *Literacy for all students: An instructional framework for closing the gap* (pp. 35–56). New York: Routledge.

Reimer, J. (2008). Learning strategies and low-literacy Hmong adult students. *MinneWITESOL Journal, 25*. Retrieved from: http://minnetesol.org/journal/index_vol25.html

Rockwell, E., & Gomes, A.M. (2009). Introduction to the special Issue: Rethinking indigenous education from a Latin American perspective. *Anthropology and Education Quarterly, 40*, 97–109.

Rodriguez, B., & Olswang, L. (2003). Mexican-American and Anglo-American mothers' beliefs and values about child rearing, education, and language impairment. *American Journal of Speech Language Pathology, 12*, 452–462.

Roessingh, H., Kover, P., & Watt, D. (2005). Developing cognitive academic language proficiency: The journey. *TESL Canada Journal, 23*, 1–27.

Rogoff, B., Moore, L., Najafi, B., Dexter, A., Correa-Chávez, M., & Solis, J. (2007). Children's development of cultural repertoires through participation in everyday routines and practices. In J. Grusec & P. Pastings (Eds.), *Handbook of socialization* (pp. 490–515). New York: Guildford.

Roller, C. A., & Matambo, A. R. (1992). Bilingual readers' use of background knowledge in learning from text. *TESOL Quarterly, 26*, 129–141.

Roskos, K., & Neumann, S. (2011). The classroom environment: First, last, and always. *The Reading Teacher, 65*, 110–114.

Rothstein-Fisch, C., & Trumbull, E. (2008). *Managing diverse classrooms: How to build on students' cultural strengths.* Alexandria, VA: Association for Supervision and Curriculum Development.

Ruus, V., Veisson, M., Leino, M., Ots, L., Pallas, L., Sarv, E., & Veisson, A. (2007). Students' well-being, coping, academic success, and school climate. *Social Behavior & Personality: An International Journal, 35*, 919–936.

Sarroub, L., Pernicek, T., & Sweeney, T. (2007). "I was bitten by a scorpion": Reading in and out of school in a refugee's life. *Journal of Adult Literacy, 50*, 668–679.

Scarcella, R. (2003). *Academic English: A conceptual framework* [Technical Report 2003–1]. Santa Barbara: University of California Linguistic Minority Research Institute.

Schleppegrell, M. (2004). *The language of schooling: A functional linguistics perspective.* Mahwah, NJ: Lawrence Erlbaum.

Schwieter, J., & Jaimes-Domínguez, J. (2009). Maximizing indigenous student learning in the mainstream with language and culture. *Contemporary Issues in Education Research, 2*, 39–46.

Sexton, S. (2011). Putting 'Maori' in the mainstream: Student teachers' reflections. *Australian Journal of Teacher Education, 36*, 33–45. Retrieved from http://ro.ecu.edu.au/ajte/vol36/iss12/3

Sinclair, J., & Coulthard, M. (1975). *Toward an analysis of discourse: The English used by teachers and pupils.* Oxford, U.K.: Oxford University Press.

Souryasack, R., & Lee, J. S. (2007). Drawing on students' experiences, cultures and languages to develop English language writing: Perspectives from three Lao heritage middle school students. *Heritage Language Journal, 5*, 79–97.

Sousa, D. A. (2012). *How the brain learns* (4th ed.). Thousand Oaks, CA: Corwin.

Spillich, G. (1979). Text processing of domain-related information for individuals with high and low domain knowledge. *Journal of Verbal Learning and Verbal Behavior, 14*, 506–522.

Spring, J. (2008). *The intersection of cultures* (4th ed.). Mahwah, NJ: Lawrence Erlbaum.

Spycher, P. (2007). Academic writing of adolescent English learners: Learning to use "although." *Journal of Second Language Writing, 16*, 238–254.

Stewart, S., Evans, W., & Kaczynski, D. (1997). Setting the stage for success: Assessing the instructional environment. *Preventing School Failure, 41*, 53–56.

Tarone, E., & Bigelow, M. (2005). The impact of literacy on oral language processing: Implications for second language acquisition research. *Annual Review of Applied Linguistics, 25*, 77–97.

Tarone, E., & Bigelow, M. (2012). A research agenda for second language acquisition of pre-literate and low-literate adult and adolescent learners. In P. Vinogradov & M. Bigelow (Eds.). *Proceedings from the 7th annual LESLLA (Low Educated Second Language and Literacy Acquisition) symposium*, September 2011 (pp. 5–26). Minneapolis: University of Minnesota.

Tenenbaum, H., Visscher, P., Pons, F., & Harris, P. (2004). Emotional understanding in Quechua children from an agro-pastoralist village. *International Journal of Behavioral Development, 28*, 471–478.

Tharpe, R., & Gallimore, R. (1991). The instructional conversation: Teaching and learning in social activity. Berkeley: University of California Center for Research on Education, Diversity and Excellence. Retrieved from: http://escholarship.org/uc/item/5th0939d

Toohey, K., Waterstone, B., & Julé-Lemke, A. (2000). Community of learners, carnival, and participation in a Punjabi Sikh classroom. *The Canadian Modern Language Review, 56*, 421–436.

Townsend, J., & Fu, D. (2001). Paw's story: A Laotian refugee's lonely entry into American literacy. *Journal of Adolescent and Adult Literacy, 45*, 104–114.

Triandis, H. (1995). *Individualism & collectivism*. Boulder, CO: Westview Press.

Triandis, H. (2000). Culture and conflict. *International Journal of Psychology, 35*, 145–152.

U.S. Census Bureau. (2012). Population—The 2012 Statistical Abstract. Retrieved from: www.census.gov/compendia/statab/cats/population.html

Usnick, L., & Usnick, R. (2009). Utilizing a writing rubric in the introductory legal environment of business course. *Southern Journal of Business and Ethics, 1*, 152–160.

Vaish, V. (2008). Interactional patterns in Singapore's English classrooms. *Linguistics and Education, 19*, 366–377.

Valenzuela, A. (1999). *Subtractive schooling: U.S.-Mexican youth and the politics of caring*. Albany: State University of New York Press.

Van Allen, R., & Allen, C. (1967). *Language experience activities*. Boston: Houghton Mifflin.

Vinogradov, P., Linville, H.A., & Bickel, B. (June 2011). Digital stories as student-centered collaborative projects. *TESOL Connections*. Retrieved from: www.tesol.org/s_tesol/tc/index.asp#feature2

Vygotsky, L. (1978). *Mind in society: The development of higher psychological processes*. In M. Cole, V. John-Steiner, S. Scribner, & E. Souberman/ (Eds. & Trans.). Cambridge, MA: Harvard University Press. (Original work published 1934.)

Wade, S. (1990). Using think alouds to assess comprehension. *Reading Teacher, 43,* 442–451.

Walsh, S. (2002). Construction or obstruction: Teacher talk and learner involvement in the EFL classroom. *Language Teaching Research, 6,* 3–23.

Walsh, S. (2011). *Exploring classroom discourse: Language in action.* New York: Routledge.

Watkins, D. (2000). Learning and teaching: A cross-cultural perspective. *School Leadership and Management, 20,* 161–173.

Watson, J. (2010). Interpreting across the abyss: A hermeneutic exploration of initial literacy development by high school English language learners with limited formal schooling. Unpublished dissertation. University of Minnesota.

Wells, G. (1993). Reevaluating the IRF sequence: A proposal for the articulation of theories of activity and discourse for the analysis of teaching and learning in the classroom. *Linguistics and Education, 5,* 1–38.

Whitescarver, K., & Kalman, J. (2009). Extending traditional explanations of illiteracy: Historical and cross-cultural perspectives. *Compare, 39,* 501–515.

Wiltse, L. (2006). "Like pulling teeth": Oral discourse practices in a culturally and linguistically diverse language arts classroom. *Canadian Modern Language Review, 63,* 199–223.

Wood, D. (2002). Formulaic language in acquisition and production: Implications for teaching. *TESL Canada, 20,* 1–15.

Wrigley, H., & Powrie, J. (2002). What does it take for adults to learn? Creating learning opportunities that support literacy development and second language acquisition. CyberStep. Office of Vocational and Adult Education, U.S. Department of Education. Retrieved from http://lincs.ed.gov/cgi-bin/nifl/combined_search.cgi?mode=material_detail&id=12839

Yeh, G. J., Kim, A. B., Pituc, S. T., & Atkins, M. (2008). Poverty, loss, and resilience: The story of Asian immigrant youth. *Journal of Counseling Psychology, 55,* 34–48.

Zacarian, D., & Haynes, J. (2012). *The essential guide for educating beginning English learners.* Thousand Oaks, CA: Corwin.

Zubair, S. (2001). Literacies, gender and power in rural Pakistan. In B. Street (Ed.), *Literacy and development: Ethnographic perspectives* (pp. 188–204). New York: Routledge.

Zwiers, J. (2007). Teacher practices and perspectives for developing academic language. *International Journal of Applied Linguistics, 17,* 93–116.

INDEX